SOMAPOETICS

All things reversd flew from their centers . . .
William Blake

SOMAPOETICS

Book One

GEORGE QUASHA

THE SUMAC PRESS

Fremont, Michigan

Grateful acknowledgement is made to
Io (ed. Richard Grossinger), *Red Crow*
(ed. Thorpe Feidt), and *Llama's Al-
manac* (ed. Linda Parker), where ver-
sions of SOMAPOETICS Book One
have appeared; and to Jim Austin of
Sumac Press, who typeset and cared
for this book on its long journey to
bed.

Cover: The convex mirror (a gift from
Robert and Helen Kelly) bears the in-
scription: *VISITANS INTERIORA
TERRAE RECTIFICANDO INVEN-
IES OCCULTUM LAPIDEM.* Photo
by Charles Stein.

preface

Eros also has its Intellect. I would speak to that in Quasha's
Somapoetics. There is a pleasure in it that is thinkable. The
arguments of lust have too often confuted growths of logical
structure. Here they con/foutre each other, twine around, somewhat spin. Of the several longer structures being sung these days,
Quasha's seems among the clearest, most vexed, funny, even
in a way duplicit (but then song of its nature tends to enthymeme)—
it revises itself, it hides dappled among its many sources, it darts.
But I think of the ogives of its aspiration, sharp slits in the apparent
substance of fact & theory through which Quasha displays, often
enough to my taste, exciting & logically voluptuous enactments.
Depth & depthesses. Our sense is grateful for the heat. Like all
hot books, *Somapoetics* writhes in friction. I poise my native Fire
here, though Q's interlocutors are nymphs of an opposite Element
who teach the subtler frictions, musculature of water. To my sense
of it, this present time is focused on the new possibility, perennial,
Osiris restored from his long dismemberment: the long poem, long
song, long count, possible among us. Of all the long processes now
going forward, I feel *Somapoetics* of the most interesting. It touches
me close.

Robert Kelly

For Arvie

and

For Susan

MAP

SOMALOGUE

I had intended to offer the reader an account, first, of the specific circumstances out of which this composition grew and, second, of the Argument of the work, according to the practice of ancient authors. However I find myself faced with a dilemma. When I consider the first of these, the "origin" of the work, I am like a man who stumbles thru a house of his own making in search of the lost blueprint; the man checks his diary and finds that his rendezvous with the architect is listed as occuring some years in the future. Thus to speak of the genesis of the work would be to embark on a journey that no sane man dare impose on his reader. On the other hand, when I consider the second of my intended accounts, the Argument of the finished product, I am like an architect gazing at a house he has built and wondering which three out of four available blueprints can usefully be applied *today*. A familiar situation in our "Aquarian" age, but not one I am comfortable in. And yet isn't it so that even the most "genuine" architect sometimes likes both houses *and* blueprints? If I were an architect, I would be of that kind.

So I've occasionally been tempted to draw up a plan of at least Book One, to aid the reader along what sometimes seems a very clear pathway. But the instant I sit down at the typewriter or sketchpad I hear a sort of "voice." It says: "Fool! Do you think to give away secrets you do not know?" To be caught redhanded in this way is like they say a humbling experience. One feels exposed. One willingly returns to the expectation of receiving mere "metaphors for poetry"; that is, as against making claims about the Universe in order to speak "with authority" on the works one executes. And yet I hasten to ask: can one trust this important task of self-description to the linguists, anthropologists, psychologists, literary critics, and the like? At this point in my intrapersonal dialogical situation, the "voice" returns to say: "Of course not, you fool!"

I begin to get the point.

If I read the message right (and I do not pretend to do so) then I'm free to tell at least this: If, as modern logicians contend, it takes two to tango, then, when the poem says One Two Three, I may or may not say Four.[*] In other words we are given to understand that despite the pressures of this idolotrous age we are allowed a certain "prerogative of torsion." In poetic terms this vine-like freedom of choice implies a way, as Milton says, of permitting the "sense" to be "variously drawn out from one Verse [i.e., "turn"] into another, not in the jingling sound of like endings, a fault avoided by the learned Ancients both in Poetry and all good Oratory." Some may find it a little presumptuous that we expect to recover such "ancient liberty" and to deliver ourselves of more than one "troublesome and modern bondage." To these suspicious individuals we can only say: You are correct. "Certain presumptions are very definitely being made, even if I cannot spell them out in a blueprint," says the aforementioned architect.

Thus I ought to apologize for being unable to satisfy that minimal expectation in every honest modern reader, namely, that of hearing a straight forward personal account of the meaning of the poet's work. I can speak this morning neither of the origins of SOMA-POETICS nor of Her Argument. Woman is Change. She says: "Write me a poem in 99 cantos that makes my wardrobe feel like new for 99 days running." She says it in such a way that one takes Her desire as a sort of courtly obligation. To hear her voice is half to believe that the 11th century and the quatrocento and the 16th and the early 17th and the late 18th are just around the corner, talking it over. Any moment now they will decide: "This time we'll get it right." And, lo, they do it, and reveal to the world that we the poets are still the first to get the news. Etc.

I have provided a sort of Glossary at the end of the book for those who find certain key terms strange or incomprehensible and whose own dictionaries fail them. A dictionary is a kind of woman, and I sometimes think our poems are written to that kind. She's hard to impress, harder to get into. She wears our jewels around her ankles to test them on her lowest lovers.

---

[*]See below "A Note on Counting and Knowing What Counts."

The reader who has trouble "getting the picture" in SOMA-POETICS may find it helpful to regard these poems as proposed illustrations for *The American Heritage Dictionary of the English Language* (1969). Thus if you look at the facing pages 824 and 825 of that marvelous wordbook (from *Messiah* to *metanephros* and *metaphor* to *meteor*), you can hardly help seeing a sort of Ideogram, or rather Tetragram, for the self-interfering brain behind the Mother Tongue. One watches the leap from picture to picture, intersecting the shuffle from word to word, and eventually one thinks: Metapoetry! And so it is: *metamorphosis* as 6 snapshots of the monarch butterfly from egg to adult; *metacarpus* as outstretched hand within which the wrist "turns into" 5 white bones; *meteor* as 6 photos (taken at 24 frames per second) from a T.V. monitor in 1963; *metacenter* as a diagrammic ship showing the "intersection of verticals through the center of buoyancy of a floating body when in equilibrium and when tilted." Now we note that *metasomatism, metastasis* and *metempsychosis* are not explicitly illustrated, nor for that matter are *metalinguistics* and *metapsychology*. And yet—long Wittgensteinian meditation on these two pages has led me to wonder whether the unillustrated terms aren't somehow active in the "metastatic" jumps, the "sudden transition from one point to another" like unto a "geological process." Consider the implicit story in the alphabetical progression of images: An egg cracks, and the queenly butterfly counts to 6 and flaps her wings vigorously; a transparent hand waves its bony pentagram in greeting; a "shooting star" appears overhead as a hexagrammic luminous trail; a wobbly boat, obedient both to "buoyant force" and "gravity," half-heartedly tries to follow. If this ark gets to the next page, it might encounter *metonymy* or *Mexico,* but what are the chances of reaching, say, *Venus*?

Now if SOMAPOETICS be viewed as a would-be "illuminated ms." of our dictionary, then one might suggest the following equation as expressing the meaning latent in the above:

Sophia in a star-car =
the hieroglyph or spangled banner advertising a new way to travel.

One ad says: "Learn to write while you ride in the astral light" beside a picture of a green fountain pen that looks like a vine. Another:

11

"Learn the Art of Levity, or Lifting the Lady's Skirt, or Making
Things Levitate by Verbal and Numerical Means" beside a photo
of a nude beauty conjuring the American Heritage. The book
sprouts wings, designed by Leonardo and the Nolan, and begins
crossing a deep, very deep blue sky being painted by Jan van Eyck
and René Magritte. On the horizon a sign appears, bearing the words:

> *There is a god*
> *Whose sole function is to say:*
> *"Read all of it*
> *Or none of it."*

At this point we give each other knowing looks and decide to do
our will.

SOMAPOETICS 1 *first series*

On the rim of the black
hole, nowhere
known, the woman by
or from my side re-
minds me how long we've been out here
looking for the object of our in-
definite need, when
out of the *blue* -- the color hovering
over the hidden fires of
volcanic forges -- a voice "arises" --
as the sun and moon are said
to do in their gradual and spectral crossing
over our heads -- saying:
Hold your hand up to the light-
bulb while retaining
your seminal thoughts: trans-
luminous relations
or the supersensual glance
at the flesh shows
the color of your kin-
ship, climb aboard when ready to
body forth.
                Now I AM
an honest man
whose habit is careful observation
but we have been indeterminately about this
walkway thru green woods or
waterway thru words like *Sea*
of . . . . -- It appears that names
are what we are waiting for, or a species of
"lognosis" has been promised us, but is it TRUE,
as it is said, Whatever led to this
is part of it, and, if not, then whose trans-
mission is this
gapped sentence
and futhermore who handed me this rootless
changebearing *soi-disant* Instrument
of Esemplastic Mushrooming?
A silence encircles me like the Mohave.

SOMAPOETICS 2

When Venus romps with the Scorpion and
Luna tips the Scales,
the sophianic ghost of Ibn 'Arabi
sings to America's heartland:
     APPLE-EATING IN HYPERSPACE
Take this green flesh, its
red veins and white interior into
your stoma: Keep Her there, She
who delights to remain, Kin, a
Woman who happens to mother
you -- for no reason but the present one,
known, poetically, as APPLE and SEED.
Half-green, half-red in the outer view,
half-sweet, cool at first, then hot and bodily
in your mother-tasting mouth: the
mantram is the shape She gives the tongue and
Now you are ready
to know the secret of the
Oedipus myth: viz.,

          She lets you in Her when
you come disguised as Man, King, willing
to be a Killer of Kings, self-
mutilating and fish-eating iconoclastic enemy
of the Taboo Against Knowing
the Art of Gnawing the Pomegranate.
The principle is simple:
Ride slowly the fleshy vehicle of names
thru all quarters of our kind nation.
At the core of town, accept
one residual glow at a time.

SOMAPOETICS 3

By the shores of Lake Leelanau,
by the rushing waters
of the brain
of Lake Michigan, north
of Grand Traverse Bay,
under the geophallic pull
of the Upper Peninsula,
                              Superiority
as the body aquatic
bounded by female nodes,
the angelic and nucleic torque of
                              Copper Harbor,
waves sucking the edge of land.
The place was our limit, or we knew
by staring into the deathly vaginal pool
the meaning of that call to dive, naked, all the way
in those icy waters. And we did it, and heard there
the voice of Mullah Nasruddin:
              A nail is like a requiem,
he said, and a man much of his bearing
trespassed our dreams to say, the accent clearly Mohave:
"I have built my house with requiems," whereupon he danced in a manner midway between
Konya dervish and delphine leaping, his
four arms of Shiva the mudra of four
in our genes, and his moving discursion
went this way:
              "Death is like a two-by-four,
it hides us in the missing three of tree-stumps.
And hearing this I scratched my skull,
quickly beat my Buck knife into a plowshare
and ran it over the seductive bones
of recent dead folk, those who dwell
in the dark of our pity.

A neat trick for dealing with brittle histories
that cling to our lives like the voices in
Mozart's *Requiem Mass,* telling us
Christ is the ultimate authority on nails,
those three iron jewels in the crown of Ogun, Martial
god of Yorubaland.
                    The latter we trust as the power
to obtain our neighbor's cow; the former,
as we are learning to trust
the burnt boards of a heretical church
to teach us the meaning of politics,
or the serpentine mound of Louden, Ohio
to teach us the lessons of history
and self-preservation,
or the printed stones of David's sling
to teach us the use of phrenology,
or the narcoleptic desecration of
rice fields and foreign bones to
warn us of the triad of power
in the pen, the penis and the pistol.
And this we will know when we know
that ink is seed
and seed is fire
and fire is
wine for the Last Supper
such as Mozart drank during composition
of his *Requiem Mass,*
incomplete
but in his knowledge of
forthcoming death."

SOMAPOETICS 4

I'm a stranger here myself.
Hence the alternating willingness and reluctance to
follow these voices large and small, but can these gods be
more than these functions? Silence
to my questions. I imagine a Bard or
he imagines me to say: *Circumambulate*
as you listen, and execute your drawing as a cross
between an open geographical mouth
and a nine-pointed circle of black stone. Got it?
"Yes and no," I said, but the Recital rushed on,
harmonious surfic clash and a
weird kind of timing, the
importance of knowing the right moment means I
might be your Master, or maybe you're
mine, and I'm the Guide
thru the hell of your making -- Clear
as Negative Space, I thought, *where*
you will notice the inward dwelling of Seven
Masters of the Mohave, and their Masterful Women makes
Fourteen to reckon with -- say, that's the date
of my birth, 7th month, 14th day, it's gotta be
mine to hear thru, *you are its*
to hear WITH, con-
spiracy of our mutual breathing to voice the fires of con-
fusion: I said circumambulate
as you listen,why do you stop to war
with our ways? the Black Space opens
to the Will to Open
together your female waxing ears and the
Purple Jesus of your wining lips to
break into fleshy song O ELIJAH! O KHIDR! where-
upon you may find yourself transported into wandering
from, say, Andalusia to the Middle Orient, carrying
back your Keatsian allegory or forward your fire-
side reverie, wearing your flash-
light in your mouth
of magenta: SOMAPHANY
> *The morning-red shape on the night-shade*

SOMAPOETICS 5

"A man of immense desire
visited us here in the Center of Heat
and solemnly requested use of the Mohave Vine,
Active Genius of this place.
Our Seven Voices told him of its power
to obtain all things possible to be believed
and to perpetuate endlessly the reality it serves.
And we emphasized "reality" as meaning
what a man makes it
and what in turn
makes a man the particular
tub of water he or she is, twisted
in whatever figleaf floating on top
in full view of the horny gods.
Thus a caveat was in order:
AS YOU USE THE VINE, SO WILL IT
USE YOU. Read it up or down
it's you reading it.
Furthermore, all tongues operate in this way
including of course that of Earth
whose saliva is liquid fire,
moisture for Her Potters -- they
whose brains are kilns
and whose hearts are vats of glaze.
And lest the Figure of our warning go unheard
we add: It will hang
you by your own desire
if yours is weak enough
to breed pestilence: IT
will be satisfied, if not by the
everready cock of Earth Herself
then it will eat your sex away.
But our visitor would not be frightened by
threatening wisdom-as-such. So goes it.
'I'll USE the Vine,' he blurted to the American sun.
And so we granted him his handful of torque.
Whereupon he began in earnest to spin his web of desires:
'A case of Chateau Lafitte-Rothchild 1959.
A carton of Camels and a butane lighter.

Head Chef from Le Procôpe, an order of *cervelles en matelote,*
and a castle in walking distance of Mont Ségur.
In the dining room: a Tintoretto *Last Supper*; in the main
bedroom, left of 14' X 34' bed, Van Eyck's *Arnolfini Wedding.*
One albino falcon, four churring Mauri crested honeycreepers,
songs of the Humpback Whales, the enchanting "My Lady Cary's
Dompe," the latter to be played nightly on a Henry VIII spinet.
And most pressing: evolved specimens of the following yoginis
skilled in Tantric sex magic: Kamchadal, Provencal, Balinese,
Chilean, and Columbus (Ohio). We pause.'
Request was granted in four minutes and ten seconds. AND
the man leapt like a dolphin at his many treasures
somewhat in the manner of a faulty metaphor.
Alas, hardly had he carried this elegance beyond
one glass of Lafitte and the warm breath of the Cathars
when in the distance a VINE was heard, nutating
anxiously about its triple staff, generating
                                        GREATER NEED.
And it made the very ground to quake
under the man, and left him limp with fear and trembling.
No doubt you have guessed the follow-up:
He turned tail and fled back to us
and wept and slobbered and begged us to release him.
Most unpleasant to see the manchild thus to despair BUT
we refused.
Instead we instructed him as follows:
                                        Direct the Vine
to pursue that dog over yonder.
And see that tail? Direct the Vine
to straighten it and KEEP it straight.
So did he. And the dumb and directionless vine
slunk its sleek and omniumgathering belly across our
granulated land, and gripped the curl
like a guilty serpent's tongue, and straightened it.
The job done, it naturally returned to its own circum-
volution about its axis, of necessity but unwittingly releasing the dogtail, which in turn recoiled, obliging said
Vine again, etc., which organism found itself occupied
in a system of changeless change.
Our Hero was SO relieved
by his new freedom, he barely heard our parting remark:
    The mind is like that dog's tail."

SOMAPOETICS 6

That red-headed
Balinese yogini who
slips away with
the morning in her hair
cries out to her suitors, the poets
and critics--as if to test
mastery itself --
              and paraphrases her
Odyssean hero:
              "In *my* bedroom,
no one allowed who doesn't know we read
for power,
             the book
             a ball of light
             pausing in our hands.
Consider the Chinese
who like very much to state their ideas in couplets:
    All streams flow, the mountains are not moving.
    White clouds move on, but the blue mountains move not.
Now, who among your mental jocks can follow
the quick white words
leaping from the great blue tongue
                           clear thru
apparent death in the lost third ear?
You think I but sport with you, Balinese style, no?
Well, my lovers, I offer you unlimited excursion in my
white desires -- Join me behind the
blue door -- Look, even now I open
the Cruel Theater of my Oriental thighs!
Correct me if I'm wrong, but aren't you wondering
if that infamous door exists? Allow me a couplet:
    Absolute presence of mind in a tough situation:
    The blueness of the door."
She lost us, or we barely noticed how
she disappeared like sulphurous
sheen
      participating
our dark
glasses.

SOMAPOETICS 7

Dawn notches the horizon
or the bloody finger points out
its Goethean Theory of Color: The trans-
lucent eyes of our barely revealed Cathar beauty
astray on the surgical sands of Mohave.
This much I claim to understand of her:
that she has walked the living roads from Montségur,
that her voice is as a veil that closes on what it finds,
that she "knows" Arnaut, the Nile, and "where the sun
rains": *Tro lai on lo soleills plovil—*
My eyes snag on her physiological rose, the quick trans-
mission, a newscast of: *DIANA*

Marsmaid a-
Stride Her leaping dolphin
Dreams of light, mountains, forests   For no reason
But that it pleases Her
The ancient animations   The central "purpura"
Of hemorrhaging Earth   Are points
Of culmination and   These simple actions
Of sun-light   Entering
Her wine-stained veil

*   Such are the colorful facts*
Or the facts of color   Such is physical history
The interior nature of a clay vessel filled to the lip with
Anterior flow of menstrual time

*   Diana is Woman knowing*
You in the manner of your knowing   Trajection
Loinclothed catalogue of   Fleshly mantra
Target of lengthening tongues
*   In the Telling of Her Temple at Lake Nemi*
Initiates milk a secret incarnadine fungus
And from "The Churning of the Sea" AMRITA
And in Her Bear-hands the terra cotta flagon
And She thrice-brained in the seventh of the thirteen months
And calls the lusting Dove into Her Oak
And Heavens spin
*   On Mount Mandara*
*   "Good Lady," sings Peire Vidal, "I think I see God when I*
Gaze on your body!"

SOMAPOETICS 8

Turreted shell, long-spired gastropod,
Imaginacrux of Mont St. Michel,
The timely twining up thru our City
Linking the lower female mouth
And our risen manly lognostic flair. . .
So it seems to us, as we sit here gazing at
this found object, cast into the garbage by
Nizam, the housemaid whose petulance expresses itself as
the gaudy scientia of conchology and theodendrology: her Writ
of habeas corpus cum causa claiming the aforementioned belly-
footed creature, that proud slug,
cowry, limpet, or any ventral muscular mass
serving as organ
of locomotion -- crazy music
that leads us like a woman.
The fair princess has this to say on behalf of shell-life:
"From Primal Stupidity we arose
—i.e., out of the morass of Presomatics—
first thru the use of certain beastly devices
and later thru the transposition of these into somatogrammic
crossword puzzles, containing that lovely sufism [horizontally]:
Every stick always has two ends!
And running downward that equally charming virtual focus:
Being's level [crossing thru *Every*];
attracts [thru *stick*];
the [thru *two*];
life [thru *ends*].
In one exegesis, you may be interested to know,
the reader, or puzzle addict, is himself
the one walking thru the woods, and
characteristically checking his heels for dogshit
he suddenly finds his hand is being held
by an irregular stick. Or let us say
he has been handed an obligation
by no means unspeakable."

22

SOMAPOETICS 9

"Assume that we belong to an ancient family that was entrusted with a Secret sometime in the 16th century. The Secret has no name but has been called, by certain relations, 'Vril' or 'the Odic Force' or 'Eos-Estella,' although even the most stupid cousins know that the name is a fiction. And these individuals are also party to the knowledge that the Secret presents itself as a 'quality of light' at the point of becoming sound under water. Those who have heard the radial songs of whales have been known to ask in private whether there are not some whales in our family. No one knows the answer, for the only authentic remaining document bears the brief inscription:

> TELL A TALE THAT KNOWS
> IT IS A TALE THAT KNOWS

This is strange business. No one is certain who anyone else is. We sit around telling learned tales but no one knows for sure whether he has met the stated requirement, although it sounds simple enough. Sometimes we debate whether this or that story actually contains the Secret, but we always end with a 4 to 3 difference of opinion in a situation where 'majority rules' proves nothing. Yet we do know this much: That as members of this body politic we are permitted to function in any organic manner, such as gazing with erotic pleasure at a brother's wife or else thinking 'aloud' in skeptical delight: What does the mind show iteslf when it shows itself the family Secret? For most of us do admit that the mere asking of this charged question produces in us, if not direct knowlegdeof the Secret itself, at least a sort of 'family feeling.' A heartfelt pang, if not fullfledged cardiognosis. A kind of debt, admittedly vague, even remote, but a debt nevertheless, as when one borrows garlic from a neighbor, and forgets to return it, one carries around a 'garlic half-memory.' One has garlic nightmares, and so forth. It is almost as though one had promised and been promised, source unknown, what cannot be articulated, except perhaps as: *A Star is the subject of this song, such as Solomon sang in the Shiar Ha-Shiareem—"Your lips alembicate Amrita / Your cheeks halve Pome-granets / Your hair gathers the goats" etc.—indicatively present and subjunctively known, were it ever anywhere other before now,*

Lightyears away .... We identify it only as what cannot but be happening, since we know it in our family, and it is written in our album, and dated. The Autumnal Equinox approaches in this the Year of the Rat. It seems the Making Noose is around our neck, its self-crossed knot a path that numbers our days, as though backward and along the Tail of Ceres, wagging between Mars and Saturn, 1801 be it to distract the 3 heads of Cerberus, that we enter here in search of counsel, or a quiet place in the Andes."

SOMAPOETICS 10

The Marriage

SOMAPOETICS 15 *second series*

Venus, the bright thought
slipping thru the dawn.
Kuan-Yin, among Rousseau trees,
waves the traveller onward
to the Land of Kokaygne.
Naked crepidinous women
encircle a luminous tree of fruit:
Earthly Paradise
where the Egg walks up to you,
asks to be hurled in the Great Parabola.
We await the plash,
the inevitable return to ground-level, the object
of power, in our laps --
for this Garden is a Walled Place, like a Human
Cell, and on this local screen we watch
Iroquois nail a chosen Dog, Coyote's cousin,
to an old rugged cross.
                              Howl of Orcus
from the *New York Times.* Beauty
winning the Prince elicits from the audience the cry
of Garbo: "Give me back my Beast!"
                              There are Patterns
which no one but no one can follow,
said the Siberian carpet-maker,
                              and each time the women
gazed upon the intricacy of woven lines
                              they began to sing
the lost songs of a forgotten tongue.
And once a woman with very old eyes looked into my palm
and began to hum.
Woman, I shrieked, is your medicine only a tune?
"There is a logic," she replied, "peculiar to the sound
of a virgin whistling in a woods."
My attention lapsed -- a crazy creature
was leading a poet thru her timeless caverns of splendor
upstate New York --
                              and meanwhile the woman grabbed my five
and fled, leaving only this red book
of dubious authority. I consulted it:

Venus is the power
to bind young Mars or any god of
iron and fire
        within the Page, the Zero
everywhere centered, circumferentially
nowhere --
        the Mrof, or
that which reflects your mind
in its instant incomprehensibility
at any distance.
Elsewhere in this learned Somatic Treatise,
we are warned:
        Nothing in Our Book has meaning
beyond the fact that it Works, and works Hard.
You who would follow our Concord
will wander 7 times 7 plus 9
somapoetic years
across the Mohave and down the spine
of any american dream
        until She opens.
Then we will climb
our reconstructed wavefront.
Give me my mirror, I want its quicksilver!
O orange moon of Kuan-Yin, you have touched my brain
with a hot finger, I am grabbing for you
with my four arms.

SOMAPOETICS 16

Where the Andes empty
the blood of the Pyrenees
into the Mohave, I saw
the crystalline Eos, *thought*
She poured a cup of acid orange
over an ancient carpet
to heal its broken strands, its
burnt-out passageways
leading to the lost Symsonia.
No Man, She said, *can follow*
me who can't follow his own
story --
       I almost got close enough
to touch Her nipples of red berries
or the pronged twig on a silver chain
around Her long Cranachian neck.
Freedom is an artifact,
She chuckled,
               build me a labyrinth
and I'll set you lose inside
the communicating anatomical cavities
crossing the inner ear.
                   She turned left
at the sleeping City, I stumbled after
the netted light, entering the hologram
of queynte and slimmery cortex.
Interested in history? She asked, humming
as She ran Her fingers over the intricate lace:
       Take me back to Nam Matal
       and show me the giant masculine hands
       building the islands, O
       Carolina, my Kamchadal
Like it? History as told by Sechnam magicians
of Tierra del Fuego. Or try this:
Slavonian witches now and then have parties
spinning by full moon-light on a cross-road
or assembling in the tops of ash, walnut or linden
with preference to those whose branches grow thus:

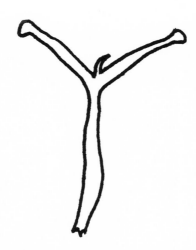

And you will perhaps have noticed, along the route from
Padua to Florence, thousands of trees, supporting vines,
trained to take this same form: Shiva's tricula
which gave the trushel or cross of the Gypsies—
especially the ash, beneath which roots of power grow,
as sings the maiden who learns her lover is untrue:
"Ima trava u okolo Save / I korenja okolo jasenja," i.e.,
"There are herbs by the Save, / And roots around ash trees."
And why do you suppose she says so?
Because she can USE it to make a Love-potion.
Seek the dunghills after dark, the caverns
within us. See the ALRAUN, image
out of mandrake.
                    You doubt what you see and hear?
To paraphrase the Gospel of John, it will come clear
in time. Here, try this.
We may eat our way to Jerusalem yet.
She handed me a *fausse-oronge,* also called *crapaudin.*
Ah but I can smell those Texan mushrooms even as I write.
I could not help but eat of the fruit. *No blame.* Re-
sistance, friction, sparks, the TORQUE!
I hear them

SOMAPOETICS 17

I see it all very clearly.
Directly before us is a long hall.
Cubicles appear on either side
as in a Paduan monastery.
We haven't been here for centuries,
I thought, wondering why.
                              The tongue is long,
but has memory failed us?
                    Memory is the veil
of my gown, and holds my breasts from you, She said;
in one room of the City you'll have the balls to rend it.
What better reason to risk getting lost
in the folds of Myth, I mused,
                              gazing into the open
mouth on the page.
Surely there is a sentence,
somewhere, long enough
to see us thru,
                    surely along this way, words
will get raw enough, the core
of the apple as dream, we
will fuck and give up poetry
for this brief night
and know the Bride
equal to our need.—
                    She must have overheard
my thoughts, for at this point She rushed ahead and
disappeared thru a jeweled door, blue,
familiar in its bearing
and questionable in its ontological status.
It refused me entry.
I was like unto a pheasant
ostrasized by a bush.
Fallen into wandering mind
I began to remember lines in old poems
and the *mrof* broke, spilling the wine,
i.e., the blood.

SOMAPOETICS 18

Dinner is served.
The walls of the castle are dank
or rather they submit to our desire to describe them
according to the tradition.
The hour grows fleshy with our speculations.
We figure
that Tintoretto "grew" in relation
to images of the Last Supper
which functioned as a sort of *alraun*
or rooted paradigm, generating endless
replicas of itself,
                              always returning,
always different,
                              Time, intersecting
all things at center
of the idea, rendering it
visible, as a vine
is an objective view of
wine, in its role as
linguistic extension of spilt red
juice, crossing the
tablecloth, liquid of life
folding in ratios of brain and tongue,
paint.

SOMAPOETICS 19

Our guests are amused and beg us to continue,
and aroused by good company we venture,
crossing our fingers:
Rodin's Thinker is a fakir,
the sort of man who would not have read
Amazing Stories, June 1947, Vol. 21, No. 6, namely,
Theodore Illion's account of the "Tibetan Shaft," leading
to 7 buildings of the "City of the Initiates," comparable to
Richard S. Shaver's "Mystery" re:evil "cavern people," DEROS.
But note on p. 136: "ALL CAVERN PEOPLE ARE NOT DEROS,
                                                        thank God!"

Relieved as I was by this bedside knowledge,
I couldn't get up early this morning as planned
because a certain recurring dream *sucked*
me into its vortex: dark
powers, or rather
the mind displaced
and allowed to function at distant nodes:
the eyesocket sinks
at four removes from my body,
becomes a shaft.
Throw in a stone,
                        wait three lifetimes for the splash.
The voice of my Bride? Next I'll be
following one of K's scarlet women into a cavern
upstate—across time-barriers
keeping us
from the true America.
I too am interested in Indians and their reasons
for living underground in such awesome numbers.
Darkness Over Tibet.
                        Note also Oak Island, Nova Scotia,
alone among some 333 in Mahone Bay has
oak trees, red clover, and certain fungi.
In early days settlers believed it haunted, told tales
of strange lights, sounds, poems on the wind.
The main mystery is the "money pit" or
shaft discovered in 1795.
The root of evil.

                    Give me a verb
equal to the torque
of the urge:
                    Yfel [OE] from *UPO* [IE], "exceeding
the proper limit": we
go too far, do wrong, or too much
right, along the road of
excess,
             yfesdrype, water
from the eaves, drip, down
into the depths of Earth I am
eavesdropper of ec-
static cries
rising from wave-crests
to circle Her Palace of
Wisdom,
             gno, we do
know too much
when we are
in the know,
                    knowing the
verb
is

        [Clearly the Thinker may be said to
        stray from our point.]

SOMAPOETICS 20

A story which though strange is certainly
true, as Plato said of Atlantis.
We have crossed our eyes, She and I,
or I and my Coincidental Opposite interlust
and Our Book becomes a ball of fire
rising from the joint Left Palm.
                                        Rival paradigms
we have seen. Won't you mix
pronouns with us, O Stony Thinker,
whose elbow wrongly fixes the knee
missing the moving mark, the one inscribed
off the coast of Acapulco, in a hidden tunnel.
Now here is the model of nonsense. Nota
the sturdiness of the construction, a monument
to what we have failed to understand.
How, for instance, the observation
carries its own reversable weight, over
the Papilla Hills (to us) and into the
Valley of Yoni, whence to the Clitoral Knob
on the Blue Door, within which there is all
we have been looking for *and* hypothesizing about
these long years on the bank of the Ganges
amongst the enlightened ones, and the starving ones,
who claim they are each other, and are convincing
about the "mysteries," viz., inscrutible writing
that crosses the "Bodily Walls of Syntax," the
thinking of ancient thinkers, meditating in
impossible postures on
unthinkable problems, e.g., PAGANISM!
And upon utterance of that word She suffers Her first In-
terminable Orgasm, and Her blue eyes cross
their hidden fleshly fingers, bearing forth
the Image, that Western Brat
Historia—Latin for Observation. Look
how Mother Clio-Erato secretly smokes Her *Claviceps,* a
fungus, called "Cock's Spur," not yet in the field guides,
those passive paradigms
in our shaking hands.

SOMAPOETICS 21

and at last I resolved to launch myself
on its bosom
and float whither it would bear me
                    [*A Week on the Concord and Merrimack Rivers*]

You who have known the spirits of the rivers and woods
behold this crevice
in the palm of my Lady's hand
and if you know the art well, pass thru
and enter Her. Enter here
and you may be our guest in Her thousand folds.
And everywhere we traveled, the land
made like invitations,
the geography of Earth,
the vales of metaphor,
fried trout on the shore of Lake Superior,
a place for fauns and satyrs,
the destiny of fishes
is ours, there is no way out
of the underwater way
into our history,
                    the whales
are dying fast,
and we have barely begun
to learn their ways
of entering the body
around which we move
in travelogue:
                    and if that body itch
in 33 places simultaneously
the man thinks he's sick or insane.
Who is speaking?
he wonders, and returns to his Thoreau:
For the great god Pan is not dead, as was rumored.

SOMAPOETICS 22

Our minds are like that dog's tail
said Shrii Shrii Sombodyjii.
I have been looking out the window all day
and I have reached a conclusion:
This vehicle is not moving.
In amazement I turn
to my left and stare deep into
that girl's crossed and bewitching eyes.
She seems not to notice the world
flying past as if astride a broomstick,
made of Common Broom, psycho-
tropia of secret pharmoco-
poeia. Is this Machu Picchu yet?
Or maybe the Treasury of Atreus, the tran-
spiring ceiling, the open stomata of Earth,
the breath of the past coming to pass? The ellipse
of my thinking lapses, and the Riemannian ribbon snake
of memory seduces me: Grand Canyon
surrounded by woods, like being at Mt. Tamalpais,
looking all the way into the distance of the woods
and fixing a tree, at its depth, as it stands
out, was like that day on the shore of Lake
Superior, across the inlet and thru the Rousseau
green, how our eyes came off
their latch, tropia or childhood in the omni-
present tropics, near Miami, ever glades
to make us glad with our days, clad in our
turning ways, swinging from tree to tree to
evolve the *exact percipient fancy,* or catch hold of a
forking branch, the point of division, never again to ask *why
is this the way,* but looking out the porthole in on the
current interior, veins of *arbor vitae,* Tiresias at large and
spieling in the tomb at New Grange, Ireland, the beehive over-
lapping technique of roof-construction: Look, over there,
3 coils interspire, cross-
engraved in rock—It leads
us on, into the distance, the doorway opening
in on

SOMAPOETICS 23

Flash of gold light: the unopening
doorway -- or is it the visible future
exercised at my personal expense?
I dreamt I was writing a book, awoke
to find it in my hands, calling itself
illegibly: *The Somapoetic Speculation.*
Crack of dawn, or in the door, first instant
of life on Earth: you drop a string
on the blank page, worship the design
until the tail wags --
                              Ta'wil
"who grieves" -- am I making this
up, I wonder, or did I *really* dream the
word. I check the map, sight
Hungry Mother State Park *and*
Braintree, Mass. But no *Ta'wil.* SO
it *is* me grieving, this Green Christ—"Objection,"
says Mr. Stein, "Call Him Dionysus." Stones
in this half-dream seem to speak by geo-
metrical projections into the flesh
of my friends. *Stop wandering
in wonder,* interjects Our Lady Logophagos,
*Now no matter, child, the name. "Study
with the white wings of time passing."*
Stalks of grain on a pilaster
mounting Her stone head.
Dare I ask if She is Goddess of Adnation?
Or what a Nabataen Dolphin is doing on the verge
of the Arabian desert? Or why my shell
is yoked to Her Egg? Or who intercalates us
in this or any Aeon?
                              She lays down the Law:
*Cobbler, stick to your Last!
Or walk on your ears.
The Dolphin leaps in the current sand:
the charge of Hamlet's surfing mill.
Confused? Permit me to quote Miss Moore, our
talkative new Librarian hereabouts:
"It isn't jumping around, it's all connected."*

SOMAPOETICS 24

And how are we put together, or what
are we putting into the contract — *I*
am listening with the King's ears, I seemed
to say, and to hear: *Put thy ratiocination*
                            into this thief-sized pot
No dice! I mean, to quote Coleridge: "We receive but what we
give / And in our life alone does Nature live!" *She*
lives as She is lived -- But who *are* you, I
interrupted myself to say, and began to feel stupid --
Foolish, as in Fool, is the word to say what honors
the sacred meaning of Meta-Tools, as: to push the Button-
wood and watch the figleaves carry out the thought
to transpire
                is to wed
                            and take the Queen to fiery bed
keeping the Engine fueled greased and
moving -- I felt my bowels beneath me like
the Image of Eternity, and thought: The Husband!
dwelling in my flesh, this being owned, as *He* seems
to work my left gonad, or make me know
in the leftness of my sex, as if to say:
Only thus is Rightness visible
as Milton's darkness
is audible -- *B I O P O E S I SSSoma's*
turn re-
verses the current, hooks
up the System as a Left-Right pro-
gressive gesture -- You mean She wants to *make* me
come crying Dogtail Dogtail Dogtail all the way home? Or:
Call him what he calls me to call him, Krepid? *Gaudh-* !
or what I call upon *last, ultra Crepidam,* lasts, verbs
its way into my will -- it changes not,
but as it changes into, our lives -- this *we* of inter-
changing I's, and I am lost, or we are together, who
or what subjects itself *here*: O Adam Appled One
in whose fields our occasions play, *and* to whom
or what we chant, in the sacred syllables of this
History: *Let not the thread*
                Of my song be cut   [*Rig Veda* II. 28]

38

SOMAPOETICS 25

There is trouble in the Heavens.
There is a great tussle in the Heart, the Seat
(the Chinese say) of the Will.
Twisted by a Foreign Hand working its way into
the Place. *Will we survive?*
I cry out of the thoughts of the Split-Head, and
Tara comes to my rescue, teaching me
in the green of Her presence the Art
of Crossing Over.
                  Later on in this cathartic Medieval Dream
of roses and vines, thorns and mushrooms, goats,
unicorn whales, uroborus, the Son on the Mountain
making from his rib a Woman, to fuck Her
in the eyes of his Mother
a dummy-like voice told me:
A meal is a meditation, a meditation a meal, a
man a monkey and more like a lamb at base of the spine rising
as vitis from cunnus crying out: Eat me
or eat with me as I eat you --
                  I have awakened
from that cryptic incusuccubus now. But it haunts me.
In my Proustian flashes there lurks a subliminal image
of ancient men in ritual stance as
Question
Answering Itself.
                And in the mudra of their fleshy wrinkles
I read: *a fire is a mental genital, a wire a distance between*
            a snake and an Indoeuropineal eye -- Who
among us knows the species
which to name is to become
ourselves --
         What goes on
         4 in the morn, 3 at eve
         none at noon but this
vehicular slant of light
self-suckling Moon-over-Water
moving vaginal lips
to speak the name   SOMA

SOMAPOETICS 26

A lesson under the Serotonin Tree
on how to eat religious figs
or figments of esemplasticity,
pear-shaped and many-seeded *ficiones*
of *Homo Viator,* his thumb thru his upraised fist,
compassionate, smiling—
                              Are we not
the vulva of this Body-Tree (I ask
in this educational dream), the self-
binding and -releasing knot, thinking
at such removes from desire we remind ourselves
to glisten in relation to these things—CLAP!
goes the Master's one hand
to wake us, don Carlos and I, to endless scribbling
in our "bed of strings," suspended
over the "place of our predilection"—so *this*
is the yoke of the Egg! we mumble, the exercise
in visual breathing: DI - AN - A
DI - AN - A, on the intake (count 4)
DI, loosed into
outflow (count 8) AN
then over the cliff of air
                              AAA (hold your ennead!)
and repeat, and each time deeper down
the shaft
until you see the face of Krepid
and the naked Cranach feminine pole
on the third step of the third terrace
gathering in the false orange cornucopia
of the third head's
third ear—
                    Listen! Susan is talking
in her sleep, to save me from distraction in some subterannean *Symsonia*
("A Voyage of Discovery," c. 1820 by Capt. Adam Seaborn,
as reported in *Walden*). She says, 3:33 A.M.:
"Your whole map   is bedded
in the route to your   house"

SOMAPOETICS 27

So I am fascinated with the pepper jar and notice
-- No, Lady, not another CASTLE!
I will NOT be painted by Gothic Mind
in four folds of subtle nigrescence. --
how memory gives way to *liatgod* Work -- i.e., my
reader's brain in a vast mirror, broken
in the fall into childhood corners-
within-corners. Admittedly I *encourage* this
unless the local residents absolutely refuse our help.
Set sail! So the larynx beckons us
to draw in the line, to pull up our fishy minds
from sleep. This is a morning song.
Still can't get the sand out of my eyes, where
in this "complex" we were together, *if* a plot
exists, *then* what? Note that the well-heated heart
has imprinted itself on empty space
like an ugly duckling. Moreover, the self-sliced cerebrum
avoids decision re: *the unseeable.* Resist this.
Only by making these decisions can we refuse
to waste our minds here, believing.
Everything exists, continues the Voice -- Voice?
Vocalis interruptus. Hold it, friend. *There is*
an awakening afoot on the Earth. Why, Sir, have you chosen
to exempt yourself? and the Maggidic K-like feeling pointed
to a distant Mango Tree, billowing mineral blue-green fumes
mingling with the rose-blossom gown of Buddha
in a 7th century hanging scroll of Wei-ch' ih, now lost.
Long dream. Long enough to reach into day. Between
what is -- and sleeping on the job.
Bring the woods into the palace, interiorly
anterior, that the oral cavity be filled full
of Letters. All things are enclosed now, as planned.
I stumble out of bed, half crazed with clarity.
Are we home? I ask. And, absurdly, *Hail Barque of K!*
Your three masts are struggling to become four.
Together we'll repair the Creation and all flawed pots.
The thread is not cut but only bisected
by projective thread after geometric thread after:

SOMAPOETICS 28

Ah memory, memory, memory,
thrice-great passion to possess
the *Blazing Star:*
                    an herb
as folk-cure for snake-bite, named
Button Snakeroot (Liatris), of the family *Compositae*
Have you been bitten by our little orc, She asks
        with a horny shimmer of light
in Her eyes—Look! the handle
of the polar star!
                    Start
        By looking at the bridge
        Of the nose. Cross it.
        It wobbles in the middle.
        Strain upon the supporting chains.
        Grip it hard, hold it in.
        Loosen, let it flow back.
        Repeat three times.
        One for each hole of the dead-eye.
        The disk is pierced by lanyards binding
        The shrouds that hold your body
        To the Ship of Death.
        Your nose cuts thru the Sea.
        Forgetfullness is the body bathed in warm wine.
        Dead center: the path of a moving member.
        Now we are aligned midway to midway.
        A golden flower begins to open its umbrella
        On the stalk of the Nose. Suction.
        We are in the woods. It is raining.
        A distant tree
        Is looking into our eyes
        Telling us its name
        Pointing to its roots
        Making us dig our hole
        Insert here   Gently now
        Release the seed   Backwardswise
          I am your woman   [Say it thrice]
          I am your woman   [Do you hear me?]
          I am your woman

                                   It is rising

42

Briiing back
Briiing back
O bring back my eyyye
To me   to me

And count it for me.
If it's all there we shall sing
Moon Over Miami together.
Look!
There go the shadows
of our forthcoming ideas.
Setting sail ahead of us
across Biscayne Bay.
If this song can't catch them
Nothing can.
Call it
Corpse Hermit Crab Herbarium
and see if it sells in our home town.
Tell the folks that a hot stone
has a fire in it, like Jacob said
climbing an invisible ladder,
counting as he went the steps of the shut-up eye.
The I sound asleep with Pandora in her box.
Patterns which no one but no one no
one making three can follow in all conscience
but Look down at the carpet and hum.
Such therapy costs nothing, promises less.
Expect none, mon ami, moon not
and we'll get along fine.
I listened as carefully as I could
but can repeat nothing of what I heard.
Bury me in the mystery of fact.
Better yet, set me ablaze like a star.
What smoulders smothers.
And so on page after page
of the flesh and blood songbook.

SOMAPOETICS 30

What we know we know in our way
the Salamander, the burnt tongue, said
to the Preying Mantra--I mean Man-
drake--or the god who holds his ears
while you talk, gazing
into the candle flame, flicker
flicker the sound of saliva
in his mouth, in your ear,
and suddenly he tells you his name
inaudibly--is this a *prayer*
I'm supposed to say each night before sleep
overtakes my desires
and puts them to better use?
Say fuck, say toad
between the legs, or nose,
of the one beholding the fire
or overhearing it
as crepitation
of leaves in the distant woods
like that lovely day on the beach in Old Field
when that stick held my hand
and shook it all the way into my personal darkness
and three days ago I came across the word *crepis*
which is a kind of sunflower, ah!
song, flakes of meaning, Experience
calls us to the things
of this intergalactic angle
and their personal paths of twining
along the crepis-lined garden
of primrose perception, namely,
what we know in our own way,
in our own day, our close kind say
Salamander regularly, Solar Mantis, eat your mate,
prey on her, do you remember now?
The fire leaps beside us
and seems to tell us to take what we have,
what we have is virgin, and its sacrifice
is demanded, or else we are not here
where the song promised to lead us
thru the woods, around the toadstool,

up to the tree with forked leafless branches,
like that day at Old Field,
do you remember now, my love,
how we frolicked, tricking
the fungus flesh
into flaking, under the Sun,
and the purple wisteria inked
our fingers and made them mark
the right direction, all things
as they should be
at the instant of
taking the gorgeous fruit --
And now
we have eaten of it
and tasted its
tawniness, and burnt
our tongues in the effort
to speak of it
in that same delight
long ago.

SOMAPOETICS 31

Why have you chosen us to speak with
or, better, why have you chosen not to speak with us?
I asked at a later stage
of the aforementioned conversation.
Because I am a fold in the flower,
answered this particular unancestral voice, *you*
are the perception of the fold
or to the extent that this is so I am
speaking with you, for reasons of my own.
Let us say that all that which you do not know
equals the propensity to fold,
whereas all that which you do know
equals the propensity to note this fact
in such a way that it ceases to be so.
And yet obscurely you recall that looking
at a mushroom, taking it into the umbrellalike
coils of the brain, the rimlike
body of a white dolphin,
does not engender another mushroom
but rather the need for its presence.
It comes, so it appears, as commanded
in another lobe of time,
such as the aforementioned conversation,
if it ever occurred. I myself
do not recall it. But I know you do
because if you don't then why have you come,
why are we gathered here together today
bending over the fountain of our Mother
Tongue, the Way Between, Midway in the Journey (ah!
Rimbaud's Thimothina, je t'adore,
toi et ton père et ton chat...)
why have we come if not to finish the
sentence, or keep it going
into the subjunctive, be it
the future were cream pouring out
of the tit of past into
the ready mouth of present. Given
the verb the flower occurs in turns
by the reflex of pure feeding

SOMAPOETICS 32

Thru the frame it is beautiful.
The glass reveals the blueness of the sacred eyes.
The flatness of the surface is a baby-cubist window
        into its inner roundness.
The same frame might be used to look at you with.
Truly you would also **be blue** in this light.
Time will tell or not, sure as Orcus, or
Three quarter moons interlock
        in the picture.
They imply a fourth
        which is no moon at all but light
        in the dome. It says to say:
Terpsichore!
        I invoke you to teach me delight.
Tree! I climb you, my hand in your leaf.
Toy! I let you play with me, flapping my wings.
Trunk! I let you bear me, desire of Pandora.
Trip! I let you make me a map, the veins of America.
Torque! I take you to be my lawful wedded brain
        and body, see how
Torque frames you when I
Touch you. I see you clearly. You are my
Twin. I long to return
To the blueness of your eyes.

SOMAPOETICS 33

To be born in addition to.
The Goddess Adnasci holds up a frame-
   like womb
   thru which I leap
   grabbing the first flower that comes my way.
In previous lifetimes I was a visionary.
In this one I am a practical man.
No point in doing the same thing twice.
Though admittedly there are times when I can't resist.
Adnasci [or Agnasci] presents Her *gno*
and you and I leap thru each other.
For every goddess there is a fool to mutter her name.
She teaches the rightness of saying ,
in a tough situation:
Your God, Sir, is a cheap imitation of my erotic dreams.
He eats nightly from the Great Wok of my libido.
Mind you we sent the Snake to the Garden for a reason:
to get some things said early.
The art of Milton, Dante, et. al. is evidence
that *something* occurred.
It will never hold up in court.
But no matter, She is calling,
I am unwell, I am unwell,
and so the menstrual rivers of Diana
are washing us with fluid time
of the uncreated. I leap back.
In the upper corner of the right eye:
the inner workings of an automatic window.
There is the spot I brought you here for [the Voice points].
Tea time? *Wipe that archaic smile off your face,*
She says, and we do it, though unaware how much we feel
like early Greeks. She dreams
an arrow, draws it.
Binds and releases. It passes thru
dead center of this spot. The moving member
of Hermaphrodite, at large once more.
Our place is an opening opening.
Add me up, I want to know
which birth this is. Hail Twin!

SOMAPOETICS 34

Plateglass blue.
When you were speaking of Satan in Connecticut
I noticed your brain was plateglass blue,
she said. And this vehicle?
We turn and hear ourselves think in unison:
It is the something in the world which is
nothing. You
are here because you are traveling in it.
Don't trip. Ride
over the crevice
in my Lady's hand.
And midway across,
think this: Three pink balls
in a chrome dome.
You grow to hate pink,
such a disgusting color,
until you realize
it is also the color of the inside
of my Lady's vaginal Queendom
which is the very castle we entered together,
in the rear dome of which a bright point
of pure pinline light centers
in a crystal, revealing a world
of nothing
but light, and
you, and the pink balls,
and the reflection of the pink balls in the chrome,
this dream or show in miniature,
within which there is a miniature of the miniature,
and here you focus: *sand*, or maybe *grain*—
the latter, a maize kernal, eaten
for New Years dinner, tonight,
in New York City, nearing 1972; the former,
the luminous particles of Mohave
burrowed by a Hermit Crab
seeking his corpse in a herbarium
surrounded by plateglass
blue, in the center of which Satan
is being described
in a perhaps slightly new light.

SOMAPOETICS 35

Suppose we got off here.
Where would we be? 34th street?
Not even. Less than that.
Infinitesimally less
than we wanted
or feared. And yet
the meaning of *to run to meet*
is *to occur.*
You can run to meet a bus
but can you run to meet a bus stop
once you are on a bus, speeding past
the Cerro San Cristòbal in Lima?
Can you run to meet the Earth
turning on the axis of her *sushumna*
or your penis, if you would follow directions
and *Insert Here,* in recognition of divinity,
the opposite of divide, and thus occur,
having run across town four times
to meet a redeyed woman
who rode across town four times
on the back of your mind --
                              Call Her
Diana, moon goddess of the Navajo sandpainting,
and celebrate her with exotic rites
during which consider this:
Suppose we got off here.
Put your hand on my cock,
She says--My God! A talking statue!
I said to myself that day in the Louvre, ten years back,
caressing Her marble ass, and moving my hand
round
to the Other Side
carefully exploring, and finding there the
Little Penis, declining
to rise, ah the power
of art, to rise,
to confuse, enables us to stay
on
around the bend

SOMAPOETICS 36

Ah! songer est indigne.
Puisque c'est pure perte!
Et si je redeviens
Le voyageur ancien...

sings Rimbaud's Old Man
as the green auberge opens before us.
This is not an allegory.
Truth does not dance as our shadow here.
Take her, junkies, one and all. Eat out her
last vestige of anagogical meaning.
Let the symbols leap to their death
from the Brooklyn Bridge—
                              Inner fungi
are working day and night in us.
Hail Twin!
              Dance freely among my organs,
the phalloids, the stinkhorns, the panthers, the
muscarines.
It is said that there is a secret tradition
of lognostically splendid
nothing. It lingers in the air
like the fart of Mani, in China.
The foulness of dreams. Why relate this?
Why does Diana run screaming thru the forests?
What is so rotten that She should be made thus
to despair? Who creates such history?
                              Who to blame?

Perhaps a Voice says:
The godhead is a mongoloid. Not, repeat
NOT, a mushroom.
Here, eat this juicy red flesh
of that forbidden tree, and all our woe—
and sliver after sliver after sliver we are touching
palms, humming forgotten obligatory melodies, these

are the conditions of pleasure on Earth, that it
flake off
from pure action of the growing stem, contact
me in passing only, the in-
finitesimally errogenous zones everywhere around the
medial porpoise,
each fraction independently
penetrating the whole number 4,
the self-destructed symbol of Body, the Hag, Mother
in our grave, the flicker
of love, this minute, the dark lotus set ablaze
by the cock of light,
O Madame put your book aside
and open this one
[our Voice adds,
handing me the present text]. Peel the brain
like a tangerine, break
into sections and eat
yourself bit
by bit, savoring each.
And from each She springs
and in each She devours you
in gourmet delight.
                    In each instant gone.
Digested and shat from Her incomparable anus
into existence, into the garden, into the problem
of mind, hummmmmmmmm, this is Her tune,
She is taking the fruit,
                    Bless Her!
I am holding Her breath lest I fail Her
and all be lost, hmmmm, the very
song I
had surely forgot

I want to tell you a faerietale.
It begins:
            as time begins, the writing
embodies a refusal
to cut down a certain tree
in Georgia. We are passing thru
White Oak, crossing
White Oak Creek, looking for
writing paper wherein the tree
has not died.
            We will build a fence
to keep these words from escaping
back into Earth
before they touch you
and you come to know
this greenerie.
            The place says: *Park your crab*
in this herbarium, don't take the keys
away with you, when you swim
after Her—
trail ink, which is blood
or juice
of this familiar red fruit.
            Waverly
Creek, Georgia, how it peaks
in passing
like hidden waves: the bodies
of these girls, this verdure,
as promised, *whom I,*
the resurrected midget,
fascinate and find fascinating.
It is all done wordlessly
and sightlessly, like these sign-readings:
PECANS
fruit
For Nuts
Enquire Here.
Patterns which no one but *gno*
himself can follow, along crepis—
lined
tablets, to write upon
and be written upon

in Glynn, Georgia, at the other end
of velocity
here on the banks
of the Little Satilla.
Litter Barrel ½ mile.
This, amigo, is my magical diary.
The one that talks back.
It tells us, turning state's evidence,
Georgia too
is green as hell.

SOMAPOETICS 38

Fancy Bluff Creek.
Several ahs for these waters
these half-open fields
and roads
and galaxies. Jekyll Island
in the distance. O Doctor, be true
to your caduceus, teach us
that trick, your snake-act, twin-
skins shed in unison.
                      From this drawbridge
in Brunswick, by the Marshes of Glynn, we are waiting
as we pass.
               My mother, named after Aunt Arvie,
was not born in Savannah, as was rumored,
but grew up there. We are 77 miles
from that spot.
               My America, mon frère, twin,
I invoke you by releasing this placenta
from the middle ear, I need you
as sacrifice to the gods
within me.
               40 bad memories a night cannot split us
further. *Who* will pass Cyprus Hill Creek
and know he is but 44 feet from the tree
that goes *yak-yak-yak,* the god
who rubs his balls in public
like my brother.
               Along this road, a big-bodied man
or a mind bearing the burden
of a vast corpus
or a hermit crab, in deep
by these many waters, seems to me
a sort of Buddha, housing the Pan
not dead, as was rumored.
               O Georgia
when will your Thoreau descend from the East
or from within the self-chaste bowels of this mud
to celebrate these gorgeous woods
and gardens of all earthly delights.

That white church looks haunted,
its stained glass
for two centuries pretending
to be stained eyes, the left one
visible from the inside
sucking us into pew-sockets, *pous*
the foot within hearing, kicks a headache
from wall to wall, and the map begins
filling out, or filling in blanks
in my unlived life.
                    Let it green
like Georgia.
                    The South furthers, redeems
itself.
        O Mother, who locked up this land?
Come, we are at Champney River.

SOMAPOETICS 39

> *Altamaha Waterfowl*
>
> *Management Area*
> *GEORGIA*

Things that do not associate with themselves
are things in the path. So you step
when I say step, or else your mind will fall
into literature. Who said that,
nodding me at the wheel, all this fog
of the past, clearing at last. The moon
was over the real Miami. It's true I can smell those
ahs back there, in that old movie,
the hand handing us
what is ours
by birthright. You know it is a puzzle
when the pieces begin to fit. Streaks of color
in the glass of sky: it is a scene
familiar in its power to present the pulp
as a vulva between fingers of Her hand
handing us our bodies. *Sweet*
occurence
to meet up with you here, She says, from behind
or at root of the coconut tree, from which this one
I hold in my hand, to say this: *krep krep krep*
my stick, your nut, in my hand, *your*
story has crossed over into:
                          Butler Island, Georgia,
to which, it is recalled, Pierce Butler and daughter Frances
came in 1866, interested in the South. Her story
of Reconstruction, *Ten Years on a Georgia Plantation,*
made this place
the burden, and her nephew Owen Wister,
author of *The Virginian,* returned
here many times.
                  Notice that ruined brick tower, the tree
cut like a green pyramid. Back further
the 3 story white house, looking like the first
ever. Royal palms. Childhood dream
after dream after dream, nodding, in Miami.

This road
once served as arterial vehicular route from the interior
of Georgia to the town of Sunbury. Is Columbus dead
from Georgia to Ohio, or has it still the
weight of hot stones
in burden on your back?
The road divides across the map,
acquires its South, like the very horns of him
who butts with trees.

SOMAPOETICS 40

Butler River.
Already Champney River is a memory
and in need of redemption, like the fact
that I bought *The Virginian* at Bolt's News
with lunch money, 10th grade, corner of 36th Street
and 17th Avenue, and now that area is like they say
Nigger Town. I return for the celebration
that none seems to know is going on
even now. We go further
down 17th Avenue, like it was always
Miami with me, and on our right I give you
the ALLAPATTAH BAPTIST CHURCH, as promised,
keep your voices reeeal low thru here, close the door,
now up these stairs is the very place
where I was baptized, aged
by pubescence and voluntarily
taking the Lord to be my personal
Savior, yessuh, never to blaspheme
or take His name in vain, though in secret
we said Fuck, Johnny and me, and once or twice Fuck God
in the ass, why? I had no idea, nothing seen clearly
in the mind—
                    Now to be baptized in the Pool
with Dr. Halderman (who later
absconded with Church funds, and resides
presently in Raford State Pen.) holding my back,
and I am ready to go under and glance across
the water, see her, the Woman, waiting her turn
with God, and she descends with his arms
into the invisible wet
and is risen NAKED, her white gown showing thru
and revealing and presently to my opening eye
her bare tit, and to my body, its rising
cock, visible now as a pyramid
of my own white gown, and I know
God did not let us down, water
is her *gno,* my Yesshua, this burden, I take Him
to be my lawful bodied savior,
                              O Pearl-Eyed One,
or so the preacher appeared from beneath the water,

59

those goldrim'd bifocals an aid at last to sight,
and walking across the waters
that woman, or her sweat painting her portrait
on the menstrual rivers of my brain,
and God came so to speak
in my mouth, and I came up
the rear end of air, left the church wondering
just which end that was, God
is a curious fellow, a sin-
uous mystery, at any rate I knew
I wanted Her, God had shown me the form
of his presence, and I, Sir,
am a godly man
or aspire to same,
in these woods.
And as we descended
from the baptismal the other day,
there we met the new minister, and he did address us:
May I ask what you folks are doing here?
And I replied: This is the place where I was baptized.
And he, impressed, welcomed me home,
and I thanked him but said I was only sightseeing
and that I, as it were, had gone another way.
And he inquired as to which, and I did reply:
I am a Buddhist with a Gnostic flair for color
and a tad of Pantarxia,
which the late Nubar Gulbenkian defined
as "Keeping people on their toes,"
and I adore all wooded regions,
conjecturing that Time may be nothing but Red River
trailing behind Diana, Goddess of Dolphins, and, say,
have you been to the Seaquarium lately? Terrific show
where the girl gets off on a killer whale.
And the preacher, hearing
the word Buddhist, cried out: A WHAT?
Peeeeeyouuuu! Where'd you ever dig up THAT trash?
And I said, Little Isis-eyed and feline-bodied voices
whispered it in a Texan wind, a tall tall tale
I can't get out of my mind.
And he, with authority:

You've been listening to the voice of the DEVIL!
Well, I said, I but opened my eyes
and my pants at once, like that day upstairs here,
and out came this peculiar juice
kinda tawny in color, and I'd say fungal
in taste, and yumyum the eating part
of me says we want more.
And he said: Show me your God.
And I said: Come with me into the woods.
And he did refuse to eat of our fruit.
And on our way out of the church
we stole the Baptist Hymnal,
from row 3, the very place
where Johnny and I used to sit,
giggling and hissing before fire and brimstone.
Such good sense. Arise youth of the new age,
and let's sing one of these old hymns,
No. 261, under *Faith and Trust:*

1. I've found a friend, oh, such a friend! He loved me ere I knew Him;
2. I've found a friend, oh, such a friend! He bled, He died to save me;
3. I've found a friend, oh, such a friend! All pow'r to Him is giv-en,
4. I've found a friend, oh, such a friend! So kind and true and ten-der,

And so we pull into Darien, Georgia,
and spot Cyprian's Episcopal Church, built
"for the Colored People of McIntosh County,"
named for the martyred African Bishop
and consecrated here, Sunday, April 30th, 1876.
Over the roof today grows the mighty oak arm
fingered like a trushel.
                              And thus appears the edifice
to be held on Earth, even as it is pierced
by vines, twining on the inside, down white stucco,
clinging to the wooded arched roof. And note too
thru the stained glass window another burden of vines
which I fancy are the green lines in my friend's hand.

SOMAPOETICS 41

I go into the next room
savoring the taste of Florida grapefruit
which quickly turns into a longing for sex.
Let's fantasize together.
In the distance a tit-shaped hill,
the nipple of which is your wife
naked in front of me. I ravish her,
and discover that in fact
she is Diana, bathing in the menstrual time
of my uncreated body, half bottled in a baptismal
and half performing at peak among dolphins
off the coast of Florida.
                    On the altar, the red
covered Bible, open to II Isaiah 41:
1. Keep silence before me, O Islands,
and let the people renew their strength,
let them come near, then let them speak . . . .
2. Who raised up the righteous man
from the east, called him to his foot,
gave the nations before him . . . .
On this spot I have attempted to write with a vine
plugged into a massive, stumpy, forked
tree. The ink is invisible
but there is a message. *Georgia*
on my Mind, as burden. Let us go then
to the Champney River, following the path out
along the peninsula. We see in number,
lodged in forked branches, out in the bay,
the Marbled Godwit (*Limosa fedoa*), crying
kret kret kret, heard here
as *godwit* (following Peterson), *godwit,*
godwit, along the path, we hear first, then see,
amidst the green, and red, vines, the green serpent
with a dash of red at center

of the head. He does not flee,
nor do we, but I suppress a desire
to hit him with my magic stick, or rather the stick
spares me the usual mistake, on the verge
of which I find myself, *krep krep,* these leaves
underfoot. By the sound we know we are traveling and,
by the beat, they are airborne, over the water—
Even here, so late, we have come to learn
the traditional names of these curious things
that fly and cure, *liatris,* plants or substances
provided from the first, ignored.
A nest in that tree out †here reflecting
a nest in the sea, a Fisherman (Southern not Yeatsian
Georgian), *There go more o' them hippie yankees—*
even now, as we enter Liberty County,
which, like Liberty City, Miami, is Nigger Town.
Buff-brown wings of Godwit,
                              soil of Blood Marsh,
names that save us
from distraction, giving us
a new burden:
Sweet veda drip-drip slowly till I bend
my tongue.
                Fix these crevices. We have attended
the resurrection, at this site, of green:
crepidinous green
is its name, says the man from the East.

SOMAPOETICS 42

For in my nature I quested for beauty
But God, God, hath sent me to sea for pearls,
sang Kit Smart to the 18th century, confined
at St. Lukes, adrift in celebration. He traveled
from room to room, in search of the promised
item. *Perhaps I will find the stone*
before it enters the oyster's body, swallow it
myself, thought Kit one day, and wrote the lines:
For the colors are spiritual. Interoception
is the process, in a world of things
piercing us, and: *For RED is the next*
working round the Orange, that bloody fruit
certainly is susceptible to abstraction,
mused "S", the Female Student, the "innocent eye"
opening in the burden, felt here.
                              The mercurial sense
of self, behind Smart's seven noms-de-plume,
a ventriloquogrammic act of notable proportion,
scales itself to the need, *For SOUND*
is propagated in the spirit and in all directions.
We enter St. George, S.C., turn off
at the Pentecostal Church.
One plastic Jesus, several enthusiastic pamphlets,
and the promise
of tongues. I get a sore throat just thinking
about those nimble godwitted
yaketyyakers: if you have the gift
you hear the message in the *VOICE of a figure*
compleat in all its parts, For a man
speaks HIMSELF from the crown of his head
to the sole of his feet,
to the terrestrial last, afoot, or standing on its own
four feet, the shape of what walks, hears
its body as a tool, kin-
ship, or what we use to get there in—

Call it by its names: genos, genes, ingenium, Agni,
O hidden fire, indigen in Georgia or Florida, mental
genital makes pregnant the Goddess Gnasci,
Jubilate Agneau, gonos, gonad of asylums
fucked that mind in its own way. Archegonium means
one egg of the moss in these trees so like
my Lady's vaginal grove.
                              The process not association
but germ-gendered, like Plato's cold, somatogenesis,
like these nations of ants before us.
                                          The Queen says:
once you get one o' these natives talkin'
in tongues, ain't no stoppin' 'em, gno-gno-gnomoning
all the way home, like they knew somethin' we don't.
The kids shor' get a kick out o' watchin' 'em,
knowin' they're nuts one and all.
The South awaits us under the vocal Earth.
For the languages work into one another by their bearings,
For the power of some animal is predominant in every language,
For a LION roars HIMSELF compleat
from head to tail, said "S".

SOMAPOETICS 43

```
GOD SAID IT
THE WICKED WILL BE
TURNED INTO HELL
```

                                    Suspended
                        from a gorgeous Oak
                        3 miles South of St. George.
                        There is
no dead wood, only
misread woods, all signs can be
read all ways, as everyone knows,
the one turning into the other
at peak of opposition, pineal
into penis, my fears
into Her desires, my poems
into your mushrooms, if you like
to eat fungus. The kind
is right if there's no end in sight
turning into the beginning
in hearing.
            Hell, Sir, means bright
in Nietzche's mother tongue.
And so, dear sign, hung there from the tree,
we like you,
will be kind to you.
Come, work
your dirty magic on us.

SOMAPOETICS 44

A deep green leaf is curling
in my mind, as if burning up
with green fire, and giving off light
that sears my lower intestine.
                              I bend over
to wash the dishes, acknowledge the fact.
When I look into your eyes
I know we are children
of the sun.
              The Sphinx basks
in this desert, his sweat rolls
from your body.
                    What do you want to be,
the teacher asked Jonathan, age 7, Virgonian,
and he wrote: I want to be a bottle of *Jean Naté*,
so I can be splashed all over my mother's body.
Only I hope my brother doesn't spill me down the drain.
Hung here,
              perhaps hanged,
                                    the head asks:
Whence come you? And the body replies:
From the East. And the former: *At what time?*
And the latter: *At sunrise, when the East was
light.*
              This space we are traveling thru has no
true bounds but what this suspension yields.
I recall that marvelous Pekinese dinner the 4 of us had
in Altadena, spiced just right, and the fortune
cookie told me: WISELY AND SLOWLY THEY STUMBLE
WHO RUN EAST. And so we set sail
across the Mohave, wave after wave of sand
particles, or grains of the lover's body rising
in steam before us. What a trip, barely
able to keep on the road, if it can be called
a road. Eon tells us to get our asses moving
into the city of willows, presumably located hereabouts.

No matter. I can tell by the tides the time is
as it must be, *dolphins in these waters*
do not stop fucking to think, and why, Sir,
why gno gno gno do you, has she no space
for your member-
ship, swimmeth away
on its way away.
                How curious,
I thought, that the crepidinous mind
should speak thus in veiled tongues.
And yet our map has a West
again today, thinking of
that Pekinese sweet and pungent fish.
We drove all night to get here on time,
shoving hard against
headwinds, aware of the possible existence
of the East.
             This exercise helps us repeatedly
thru the crevice,
               we who never remember
how we got here
in the first place.
               Look at that man
flying up from the heart
of the sea. His body
is a little Egypt.

The Sphinx
sits sweating
in the Mohave
gazing at
steamy memories
of unlived ideas
century
within century of
tropism:
    Helios
in the eye
blinding us
until the day
reaches mid-
point, the
    Sphinx
is getting hotter
by the minute
just thinking of
    My Lady
and the crevices
in Her hand's
crevices--

Meet my
Queen of Tentacles
twining a
record of these
thoughts, the
    Stream
that is passing
us I claim is
mine
if I touch it, yours
if you catch Her, my
    Lady is
at your disposal
for the Night, it's
the custom
in my Country, take a
dip in Her rivers
and listen to the song
of the one who saunters
from point to point
on the record, calling
it: American
Prophecy. Diction:
I have no desire
to go

to California or Pike's Peak, but I often
think at night with inexpressible
satisfaction and yearning of the
ARROWHEADIFEROUS
sands of Concord.
I have often spent whole afternoons, especially in the spring,
pacing back and forth over a sandy field,
looking for these relics of a race.
This is the gold
our land yields,
    confided Thoreau to his Journal,
artifacts
springing from the soil like mushrooms.
A red head, a look of being struck.
That savage over yonder has 20 noble words for *arbor vitae*--
have I 20 good ones

for the body of my woman?
       Barque. Blister. Bow. Bend
in my eyesight. Brain,
can you explore the Colorado
with Major Powell?
              The head faints
at the thought and
Wrong Way Corrigan is sung
as household hero.
              A seed or glance
of light, as Thomas Vaughan put it.
Put what?
              Life along the Merrimac.
Morning across the american plains
of my woman's body. Sweat
is juice on this
continent,
         and Canyon is rimmed
with 3 X 4 foot man-
shaped tuning forks
              8 times
8 octaves across Her
waiting.
         So take this glyph and plant it.
The *liat-god* is hiding again in old sticks.
I have agreed to be your handwriting
and persuade myself daily of the tale in all things.
Mars--even red Mars--is found here
wagging his dogtail, lounging and belching
in the aftertaste of immigrant garlic.
In one of the ancient Krepidian texts he steps aside to say:
In the Age of Horus, let the woman
be girt with sword before me. Here,
drink this lingual blood.
I take it this is the monthly message
with the smell of a seasonal fungus
ventriloquogrammicly rendered
by a vine
or snake, urgent

beyond belief, if a red dwarf
scuttles so far, the night
so cold, in such dark wood, so late
in the century.   *We've been waiting so long,*
say the Redwoods of Canyon, *to get a word in*
your narrow ear, and whisper: We're here
at the rear of your wagging tongue
in secret bedrooms
of your personal pileus.
I lay in her lap, as instructed, fingered
the ivy that stains her back, and hung on
to a sound like the rolling of the left eye:
bla-ma bla-ma bla-ma, then *umbris*
and thru the gold light glancing from her body
I thought these seeded shadows
of ideas

SOMAPOETICS 46

I.

A welling up in the heart.
The toilsome liquid rises
past the throatline and enters the brain.
All referents are dropped.
The insane, these screened ones, gather
under the trees
in this old movie, *Private Worlds* [1935].
Claudette Colbert says to Joan Bennett,
We differ from them only in that we [they?]
go further. Beautiful day
in the garden, and with the sun
glancing thru her golden hair, the girl
is sewing, and, midway in the story, Sally
[Joan Bennett] passes by, and the girl says:
I'm Cary Flint. I'm sewing.
Cary Flint is sewing. I'm Cary Flint. Etc.
And later Cary comes to tea at Sally's house and says:
I'm Cary Flint. I'm coming to tea. Etc.
And, grabbing some fruit, runs into the corner
and crouches. *This is the only way we can get her to eat,*
says Nurse. Later, Sally, her marriage falling
apart, takes a leap
down the stairs, and is found mumbling:
I'm Cary Flint. I'm Cary Flint.
This, then, is the plot. The theme
is names. Private names
for the well-heated heart.
Thus, if passing an open mirror
a man sees nothing,
he assumes it is all gone, when it is only
all there. Namelessly, the bank of names is going
bankrupt. Cary Flint disappears, the quicksilver spills,
and the sunny garden is mirrored over and over,
insanely private.

II.

What vocabulary
for today, Teacher, with which to answer
what I want to be
for you? Almonds for nouns,
eat 4 a day before noon, kill cancer
before it is even thought. The heart
has its reasons, the first being
the slimmery cortex
of the pleasure dome, geodetic layers
of the desire to remain here
and want nothing more
than this. We drink
together. The heart
is a mirror
in which I see myself
loving you,
and fall in love with the image,
which changes. I disappear.
It is as if this garden, in which we are
spending the afternoon,
vacated the spot
on which we stand
long ago. The sentence
acquires a gap
at the beginning
and the story completes itself
ex nihilo, which reason knows not
beyond the fact of our existence
who have been sent here
to test this vehicle
for its power to refrain
from reflecting
what it passes.

SOMAPOETICS 47

New wine in new bottles
being drunk by the usual midgets
in a new garden, surrounded
by poison ivy. The shortest of them asks:
What would the World look like
at the precise instant the centered mind
achieves realization of the omnipresence
of nothing?
The First replies: *Everything.*
The Second: *The dog barks*
at his dinner.
The Third: *I see a single tree*
superimposed against the clearest blue.
And noting that they had answered rightly
each in his way, the Fourth, the shortest, replied:
The World would appear
as it does now. At that moment
they finished the Lafitte-Rothchild,
the finest ever, by group consensus.
A Serpent appeared to offer them fruit
and promise nothing. One dwarf
per toadstool. Each with special powers,
twin-genie in each flask. Such,
my friends, is the knowledge
and the usage among the Kamchadals.
This is not a sales pitch,
says one of the midgets, on closed circuit TV.
Yet sometimes I think Siberian spores
be blowin' across the Hudson.
Even today, beneath the Magritte-blue sky,
I met a man smashed on Gallo.
Together we accepted the bare fact
in each step its own stumbling, he
almost fell
into my arms, snot visible on the upper lip
croaking like a punctured and disjointed toad:
These muthafuckin honkies can't see
shit on a stick. Look at that sky!
It's a Ver-me-eh!
I know. I'm a sailor,
sailed four times into Rotterdam.

Look at that sun. My name is Eddie Keith.
See up there, the clouds, NOT the cross, the tops
of those buildings. He started to sing
at the peak of his voice, so that those who passed
avoided us. [I fancy brightly colored snakes be
gathering about our ankles, as we chant:
Noisiv man you! to the eye-spirit,
for which this is the ethnopharmacologic
search.] This way, Dreamer:
    Letting my thyrsus point
the path to the water, wearing ivy
in my hair, looking
possessed by Cybele herself, half hid
in my father's thigh:
    A Savannah stone
rolls thru the halls of this morning's dream,
becomes a bust, the theme of Head
seeking a name in memory.
    The streets are lined
with lost songs. Pass the flask, Eddie.
Aaaaah bullshit, you people don't know
how to live with this sun. Christopher Street
is a luminous waterfront, listening to him
croak, leapfrogging from the juicy joints
of his members, to the present dream
of shaking off slumber, and keeping
to the story
that leafs thru me nightly.
How to follow the line
in the middle of this winding road? Steam
on my windshield from the breath of a talking
statue, half-midget, half-giant, the latter
the unrevealed part, an oak
cock growing from the center
of the faerietale
threatening to use itself
on me and you,
creating space
as the absence of croaking.

The tantra unfolds its smashed flower,
its nose running down Christopher Street.

SOMAPOETICS 48

Shiva on the Bowerie.
Oldest of ideas, barked
in "the American night,"
and the newest, refusing
to manifest here, in the comforts
of poesy. Come,
let us drag ourselves down
to skin level, move across these white plains
of talking paper, and, coming on the artery,
cut in. Listen. The body-gossips
are still at it:
        Umbrellalike acacia trees
dominate east African savannas
where gnus graze.
                Catch the tone
on the run, dreaming of 4004 B.C.: *Take me*
back to Piltdown, Baby, cries the skull
to the jaw. *Color me wet*
aquadadatinta, before I run down.
Arps are grazed around. And:
This street has a god in it
posing as solar gospel, this journey-
work, one man had wit enough to name
passing on these stars to us, winos or wights who
seek out the grape wherever, wailing
Homage to the dawn man
or the one who sleeps in doorways
and smells wood all Night, Watchman of
Woodwork. Words
of wood, now Doow
in reverse, dreaming
itself back into Earth
thru a wood flute.
Gnos gaze here
from wood lines
on the run,
unable or
unwilling
to stop

SOMAPOETICS 49

Born 1:32 A.M., July 14, 1942, White Plains, N.Y.
If I could be born once a day for 44 years
perhaps I would metamorphose into a dolphin at 4:14 A.M.,
wolfhour.
          The Earth is endlessly round
and better worn in some places than others.
There are days when I can't sound like myself
for the life of me. These are times
of the uncreated doorway of my face.
We fear the brain is tapped, and watch
what we say. It is.
Moby Dick as testament. A personal letter
begins with the rearend *K* of *Dick*
to call itself Krepid, for our amusement.
Think no thing of it. No fear, please.
He only bites words.
And wooden words at that. The kind
that do not sound like us
so much as we like them
and talk ourselves out of the forest
by chance.
               This boat has at least 3 sails
and each with a mind of its own.
One wants to write a novel
that will cure a man 4 mins. before death.
One wants the barest song
to play endlessly on the jukebox.
One wants to ride Moby Dick
and speak with him.
Will the boat split apart?
Is this rising liquid the Hudson?
No answer, but the thought:

Be led across this field, upstate, the twig
spreading milkseed along the missing path
in the present life. Which life, I ask,
confused by number. *The third*
is the number coming into mind
with the *fourth following you*
everywhere. I did not endeavor to understand more
on this occasion, having felt a new word making its way
thru the brain, seeking an organ:

STOMA:

The mouth with its tree wagging.
The vaginal lip of Diana
riding the delphine vehicle
which tells me this:
I understand perfectly well
what is being said here, *if*
that act means standing under
the fall
of lingual drops
and thinking: analysis
is a pleasant way of saying
half a coconut
is not the other
half, but half
itself. Do you hear me? The number
necessary
is one. Come
here, the roads
are icy tonight, we can't
get all the way home
on a night like this, let us stay
a while in the country. Jeffersonville.
The glazed scape of history
does not come in halves, midwinter
near these arrowheadiferous fields.

SOMAPOETICS 50

Today is Jan. 22, 1972. We
are caught in a snow storm. We
are lucky because we have
food, writes Matthew, age 7, Aquarian. *We always*
have food. It is one of the miracles
of the country. Whenever there is a snowstorm
we always have food. But we never
have water, says Diane, born under the Fish. *I hope*
you don't mind all the we's, says Matthew
and writes: *We were supposed to stay*
just a day. We have to have
wine, coffee, melted ice and
cocoa to drink.
                    The Eagle
carrying off Marie Delex, 1838,
the Alps, we read in *The Universe*
by F.A. Pouchet, M.D., 1871.
                              Oothoon, wife
of the great unreincarnated Lama
speaking once more, encyclopedically,
thru us? Has she come to this?
If the Eagle is our American hero, Her flesh
is our communion, take some, says He
who appears whenever She calls. Her chains
appear as the outer edges of this conversation,
the weight of our bodies as the substance
of Her desire. The story of this woman begins
as a faerietale waiting
to be told, permitting us the uncreated
pisciform, here, if only
I can get this fire going strong,
the "conditional" terms for which state:
          you are stranded
in the snowy body of America, She
who lies within the mirror
of ice, shielding us
from the road tonight, to say this: *Nothing*
to do but Speak
of the past, or out of it, sensing
that it could never occur

and that this state is precondition
for all that does. The impossible
dream invades from beneath. Let it.
It depends on you. To occur. Run to meet
it, slipping thru Her hands like jelly.
Remember? Vaseline, in the back seat
of my 1956 Mercury, two-tone turquoise, both
voices, hers and mine, agreeing
that there is nothing
but us, Miami, us and the idea
of speaking, meaning
that to fuck is to love in Braille, that
to make a poem is to steal yourself
out of the clutches of the godhead
half urging us
away from Her, She who
moves within us, we who are
children of the Sun, He
who demands we indulge
the inner midget, our personal thief.
Think of the one who resents the criterion of size
as a substitute for names, who sniffs the trail
of intimate immensity— a woman in white,
her long hair crossing our face in the place
sometimes called dream. He is the one
sauntering down this path in the woods,
out of the East, to run to meet us
as we stumble and stammer. Think
what you want
He wants also, but more
than you imagined, before now.
There is a point in having a head. Thus
waking in Callicoon with the Devil
under many colored flowers
in Matthew's morning drawing. The night
passes quickly, near these fields,
the faster the sentence moves
to keep up with it. Shifts
along the drive-shaft, the thought
takes shape as the vine climbs
this wooded page, blank only
in expectation. The thief
wants nothing,
takes it all, and who
is responsible for loss? Indeed what
can be lost in the garden

but names? What regained outside
but definitions?
                    The main parts of the puzzle
seem to be forming
but none of the pieces are fitting in,
says Holmes in *The House of Fear* [1945]. Here
Watson achieves his essential function,
he who knows to give answers
in constant unrelation to the facts,
he who solves nothing,
the other end
of the great detective,
he sharpens our nose on the grindstone of chance
and, at the right moment, opens us
like a Buck knife
to slice the aquadadatinted fruit
depicted on this curvy stone,
ancient beyond belief.
                    Nextdoor to us
these brightly colored american flowers.
Shades which hide names
in their gelatinous Braille
and teach us how not to look
if we would see
the range of Her eyes. Let it
rise, that liquid
seeking diction
to say, for example, Holmes is the man
who reveals the midget
dwelling in the human breast.
He who gives us Watson
gives us a toy
like this one:
                    Bird Flying Flapping of Wings
is its name, translated from the French
and derived from the designs of da Vinci.
Matthew winds it, lets it fly,
it catches in the *arbor vitae*
and provides us with the opportunity for metaphor.
This time we refuse.
Eliminate all strains on the system
by incorporating them,
cries Marie Delex, ecstatic.

81

SOMAPOETICS 51

I.

Now here is a perhaps more familiar creature.
A man who clearly has forgotten
that all this rubbing he's doing with his
tongue and cortex is tied
to the tigertail of delight.
The eternal kind
that has the feel but not the lure of magic.
[Note that it is written in the record that at the crucial moment
he almost wrote *fear* for *feel*, but smelled
himself out, 3 A.M.]
                              Look at those bulging eyes
of the nocturnal animal, the flying fox
with 5 ft. wingspread [specimens of which
in the Bronx Zoo] seeing clear thru
the plotting brain
with his delicate sound-system.
He encloses himself in the many-petalled folds
of his own body, and eats.
                              This part
of the process is assigned to *Mystery,*
as She calls herself
under certain circumstances, notably
on the outer rim of the Stoma:
                              A matter of style
which is l'homme, in the cage of his choice,
the day of rest in his mouth
dripping this red hymnal liquid. Count
the beats, if you can find them, lost
as they are in the mirror breaking
in the inner ear
stumbling along with the sentence. Dreams
are this wetness, She reminds us,
the page, or mrof, as blotter,
where it goes
no body knows
alone.

II.

Definitions at dawn:
What I am looking at and/or for in this dark room
lightens the mind and/or body
by developing this cartoon film, as follows:
                                        The present
energy is not going up but down in me
falling in slow-motion to this muddy ground
burrowing crab-like or like a corpse burying itself
to annoy us
with a thought:
                        The thing or the stuff or the rush
occurs on this spot to enrich the soil,
its yeasty rise in what falls away
from us, like milkweed seed. The stick breaks
to punctuate the talk.
                        Yet some of the people
are complaining about the quality of the performance,
as if we had some say in the matter
of quality. I for one
only work here. I've thought myself at times
of complaining to them thus: Hey you
who come and go with no delight
in mind, Baptist fleas
on the back of the twin-headed dog
wagging its tigertail.
Why is the food so lousy?
Where's all that american flesh we were promised
back in 1776? A working man
wants what is his. He asks, for instance,
Am I not permitted to ravish her
who ravishes my mind, She who dwells
in the oracular pores of shorthairs?
                                        STOMA
I have yet another question:
What are we to make of all these erotic dreams
in which buddha-bodies rub up against us?
Why is there no satisfaction at once
comparable in depth to a Texan oil well
and in surface feeling to being annointed by Daniel?
Solomon is the name of my Scotch-Irish grandfather
who looked as though he knew an answer
but said nothing
when sober.

83

III.

                Are there enough grapes
to go around? Enough vines
to encircle the news?
                Bengal children are playing
"grotesque games" with the bones of the dead, for they are
"too young to understand" [*New York Times*, January 24, 1972].
And: American bees, once Italian immigrants, are threatened
by invasion of a deadly African kind, now thriving in Brazil.
A voice arises from deep within the *Encyclopaedia Britannica*:
What is the meaning of all these constant ejaculations?
We wait for an answer, and our hero the dawn man
(who burns any book found speaking about him without giving us
voice) is heard saying thru his secret aperture:
Fire being a form of fungus, feel free
to let it spread
mindlessly. Cherish the urge where it starts,
a cut below Mystery, stomachic.

84

SOMAPOETICS 52

A small opening in an animal body.
One of the minute orifices in the epidermis of plants,
esp. of the leaves, occuring as a split between two (or more)
cells of special structure (guard cells)
and opening into intercellular spaces
in the interior tissue
so as to afford communication
with the outer air; a breathing-pore 1837.
OUD under *Stoma.*
                          I remember sitting
in a friend's house and seeing the hairy gateway
of his wife's pudendum. Thus distracted
the conversation acquired a lateral dimension
equivalent to a vampire bat's awareness of cavewalls,
the sea pounding outside in a Ryder painting,
two (or more) adulterers on the precipice
across the bay (or room), preparing
to leap. She knew
I saw, shifted
to open the road of access
into interstomachic spaces, rips
in the tissue of these mindy winging colors
on which we travel abroad
these long winter nights in the East.
Perhaps I shall speak to my friend
from within the body of his woman
where my mind gathers as in a pool
of menstrual time. We leak
back thru this straw, held in her lips.
The other half of the aforementioned conversation
occurs to us now: How mushrooms
are situations in the daily life
of the inner city. A delicious Pekinese soup,
for instance. The place spoken of is anterior
tissue, which cannot be torn but is in fact
covered over
by generation upon generation of names.

In a flash, our heads at last beneath the skirt
of Madame Mystere, and, seeing all, we lose our place
in the phonebook, the finger coming to rest
in *The Encyclopedia of the Jewish Religion,* on JOSEPH KARO
and his 16th century magical diary, *Maggid Mesharim.* Ooze
between the ears, the torque of itching
makes me scratch my head from the inside.
This figure sits on my desire: if the brain
is said to be an oyster, hiding its growing pearl,
then this inner gnawing to discover the slimmery self
is a sign.
       The slipper limpet [*crepidula fornicata*]
steps his long last into our territory
touching to show the twin valve
in the forehead is being
smothered. Set sail
on this boat-shell snail. Study
the slide in the myth as it shifts
its shape from Eros
to Bios
and back: Wisely and slowly we are stumbling
who run Here, in the East, thru this vulva
opening onto the other side. Translation:
Among the Crepidula, *active association with a female*
causes many males to remain members of that sex longer
than they would if isolated. The vigorous female placed
with another female may obtain a male mate by
biting the other in two, by securing
the major portion of a scanty food supply, or by being
better able to resist the masculinizing effects of excreta-rich
water. In time,
the newly reverted male may become the more vigorous,
develop into a female and cause
the long-time female itself to become
a male. The sex of these worms is thus highly
labile. The functional expression at any instant
depends on a complex of factors, including the degree
of conditioning
of the medium.
       [*Encyclopaedia Britannica*]

SOMAPOETICS 53

Leaping
  between two worlds
--these delphine pleasures
keep us
exploring island
upon island, gnawing
the rude Galapagos, amidst
volcanoes and beasts, the forms
that fed old Darwin's brain--
  Translation
is a strange business
  Dante spiraling
into boat-shells, a moment's
need, meaning the way
we have learned to call our names
when we would urge them
to tell us where we are
or who. Or what kind
and whether as various as the shapes of rudeness,
we the primitive, approximate, makeshift, dis-
cordant, robust, harsh, raw? *rudus*--
broken stone--
  Lyric and Satyric
teaching us to ride the waves
where these ravishing mermaids
fold their bodies into sight--
  Fuck dolphins
  and use no punctuation
  but these points and virgules,
  these verges
  of leafy crepitation, the cracking
  of sticks
  and of the shells
  of sliding eggs, in these woods,
  elided woods, in these eggs
  stirring within the mind
  of Diana, Mars-maid.
Floating down the Red River of Time.
The menstrual nights out here in the East.
Luna bears no grudges. No man
speaks better than She
who moves him, moves with him
and within him. No place
fits him better
than her fishworld.

SOMAPOETICS 54

That snail crawled back into the Sea
leading us to what was lost. Do you remember
those forthcoming ideas
we used to have, walking along the Sound
noticing the crack in the world
that runs there beside us, even now.
Eve in South Florida. At home in Frog Hollow.
It gets personal. Nothing
is never abstract, no matter
who's talking. A simple
thing, dreaming a Sphinx-eye
in a friend's head. Cousin John,
we're waiting. Hurry along.
Don't complain about the obscurities,
there's a hell-bright light for each of us
escaped cons. Limping in slippers
is a form of stumbling, which is a form
of stammering
what we know best.
What knows us best, who,
stems from this room
moving in the middle
of the journey of our crab.
That's what we call our mobile home,
Crab, because it can leap
without taking its feet off the ground.
Sometimes I get nostalgic for the First House
until I realize it too is a trailer,
as we used to call mobile homes in Miami.
Three legs shift. *The brain*
is related to thinking
as the eye is to light,
said somebody else's private oracle.
This is not to compare oracles, no more
to speak of cocksize in this town. The place
fits what opens to fitting,
speaks as if spoken to,
holding a verge
that has been handed to you
like the color red.

The space
of this waterworld works
both ways, bivalvic. We make it
what is ours, it us what is its.
        See this morning how Mercury slips thru
these gates, bats a wing
in our eye. His direction is clearly across
though from this angle it appears to be
in and down. A feather
thru the forehead
as quill.
        Across the dining room
in National Deli, recalling the snail
that led us back to what was never lost,
a woman who looks like my friend's mother
shows me the hairy gateway.
                                Let us answer

a book of ink
with a book of flesh and blood,
writes Emerson in Nantasket, July 1841.
Clearly we are living in the Age of Marie Delex.
I mean hundreds are born every 4 minutes
who want only to be carried away
by the American Eagle.
They walk the halls of the New York Public
and titillate, seeing no signs
of things falling
out of focus.
        Under the world,
in Orcus, we notice her crotch
bears the odor of those Texan mushrooms.

SOMAPOETICS 55

I.

As Amy Lowell wrote with something else in mind:
If I could catch the green lantern of the firefly
I could see to write you a letter.
I feel the wine-dark urging, and it isn't half
what they supposed it to be, or not *the*
half holding us from our forthcoming selves, but the one
uplifting the virile member wagging
within the tail of all visible things
on the lower end of which we
are suspended here.
                    The heretic foxes
have various faces, but they all
hang together
by their tails, said Pope Gregory IX.
Flying foxes, we might add, a kind
of bat, and when we dangle we dangle deep
within the blueness of Her eyes
sucking the ceiling of the cave of Her skull
and when we fly we fly out
into the dome of St. Bartholomew's Night
warming our bodies in the blaze
of burning Huguenot flesh, Aug. 24, 1572,
the scent bearing a generalized plot of revenge
on history. *History*
is an interesting thought
thought the Fool, the cerebral phallus,
outloud and called it
Art. In fact it is the flight pattern
of these five feet of wing, *or is it*
Dracula? wonders Marie Delex,
self-titillated with the snug terror accompanying
menarche. The moon begins
where the seepage shows thru as the red stain
of the blood of Our Lord, she adds
to give the thought dignity.

II.

*Is not the midnight like
Central Africa to most of us?*
asked Thoreau, stumbling
or stammering thru these gorgeous woods.
Veil indeed. The Veil of Time
is but the way it feels, i.e., the way
it knows its naked self
to be out here, where we are asking
in this cold winter,
What time *is* it?
                    *In the real
dark night of the soul
it is always three o'clock
in the morning,* replies Fitzgerald
and drinks himself back
into oblivion.
                    Marie and Amy watch
with pleasurable despair, at odds
with our wine-dark urge. We set sail
without them, appearing
to them as Jumblies adrift
on the hopeless sea, and as thieves,
rapists and death-dealing
giants. And so we are.
*Hey you! There is an awakening
afin,* we hear
across the waves, the white lines
on the blue page, the empty space
that we are filling
with time, as excuse.
                    We count to 3 and the colors polarize,
and upon utterance of the number 4 the ink
covers the page like spilt juice, chemically akin
to blood, on which our friend the vampire bat
is feeding, or taking communion,
at this very moment.

SOMAPOETICS 56

I.

The moon is nothing
But a circumambulatory aphrodisiac
Divinely subsidized to provoke the world
Into a rising birthrate,
writes Christopher Fry in *The Lady's Not for Burning.*
Diana is pleased for the morning, She who knows
something we don't re:
the demographic prospects
for Earth. *The barren wastelands*
of the Moon
may be sitting on underground pools of water,
reports *Natural History* [January 1972].
                                        We move
by leaps when we slip from place
to place, and some crackpot in the woods
is mumbling something about the direction being "forward."
Not to be believed but thought I say
in a ventriloquogrammic message
from the inner midget.
                              Dolphins
do not sleep but achieve a state of waking
for which *we* have no name, snoring our way
thru the other half of
the passage—
                    It is three o'clock
in this dark winter morning, we run
like gnus across the savannahs
and into the wolfhour:
                          The acacia
is the Tree as I
am a single unit
in this landscape. I give up
all claims to the place.
Once more the theme of names has changed
movies. *Animalized water,*
muttered Thoreau, gazing at the emerald
pickerel in Walden Pond.

II.

                The tablet
on which he writes mirrors the wag
of sensation in his stomach. He pees
in the pond, admires the change
of color as a sign of the work
of the poet, notes the swag
of temperature in the passage from medium to medium
and the shivers along the *sushumnanadi*,
rising like snores. As within
so without
this. Before this
Whatever led to this is
part of it, inscribing itself continuously
around the Grecian Urn. As *below*
so *across, by* and *therefore. Where*
and *why* have been cancelled
or rather subsumed by the category of *yellow*
entering the chemical composition of *blue*
and yielding the aforementioned *green.*
All in the light of this afternoon sun
and the evidence behind, watching the hours turn,
What's In The Brain That Ink May Character?
described by the late Warren S. McCulloch as he traces
the physiological basis of knowledge. He quotes Mark Twain's Law:
"You have to have the facts before you can pervert them. Which
are *the* facts? They are those that puzzle
us." [*Embodiments of Mind*]

                Asclepias syriaca,
or common milkweed, has pointed pods that split open to release
seeds with downy tufts, spreading along the path
as we walk and talk in the country.
                        In a flash our friend
has the flaming sun in his eyes,
and at the center the sweating sphinx,
and a feeling of the outer limits of this space
thru which we move as the condition
of being
almost more wide awake than
than we can bear.

93

SOMAPOETICS 57

This daughter of a voice,
        this bat-hole
with an echo in it,
        call it a call in a stump
and leave it at that.
        It does, yes it does
give me the creeps at times, he admitted.
An experience in the lengthening spine.
        An eye lost its memory,
wrote Eugene Jolas, an american man who set his soul
to study in a learned school. *The texture*
is threaded with Fool's Gold, want some?
asks the glancing light
as it twists thru Siberian carpets.
If you touch one end to your parting lips
remember She holds the other
between her bare legs. Want more?
seems to be the message in Her eyes, crossing
to fix the bridge of the nose
as it smells this crushed Sunflower.
Let us return to literature
where Her song is written in monthly red:
I see a rainbow-nymph
wide-spread
upon a dolphin
surge past
in the opposite direction
to the leviathan, as Harry Crosby, Sun-worshipper
dead at 31, wrote in a message to Mistress Death.
It don't make sense, I thought
finding myself thinking in the tongue
of my great grandfather from Alabama
whose name was never pronounced in my presence.
Your text is beaded with blue
and green mold, says this Southern Side, and further relates:

A MEMORABLE FANCY

As we were walking thru the richly clad hills
outside Austin, enjoying the Mother Land
of Lyndon Johnson, we happened into
a gorgeous garden at the center
of which an Ad Reinhardt green-upon-green space
like unto a man talked
thru our minds and said:
                              Earth
is the other side
of you, why have you abused Her?
Stick your nose in Her ass,
this mud under sole [I bathed
hands and face in it] , *and feel this dark ground*
breathing you.
                    The Flying Saucer
or whatever voices travel upon these days
hovered beyond the reach of eye.
I waved my hand and butterflies poured forth
like flying fate or waves of golden butter,
                MUIOPOTMOS
these grains of sand
each containing my brain,
its inner pearl, lodged
in its oyster body, which he offered me, as it were,
on the half-shell:
                    Here, eat this,
he said greenly, and he handed me
a reddish mushroom, mirroring the juice
which pours forth from the stem of the pineal
and into which I dip my quill
and record herewith the Proverbs of Orcus
out of the Delphine Stoma
or Gea's Blowhole
thru which She breathes and talks:

95

THE PROVERBS OF ORCUS

1. The Thrice-toed Mars-maid swims
in the erotic dreams of a midget
who peeps thru our window.

2. *Every Virgin was born a Harlot,*
says Harry Crosby who presently resides in Fire.

3. *Deep below your fears*
sounds the music of the gears,
cries Ashtoreth, suffering a Phoenician orgasm
and dwelling in alphabetical proximity
to *ashplant,* a staff or walking stick
made from an ash sappling.

4. Here, take this corn stalk lying across
your face, its inner walls are shreds
of structure, which bend and twist
like a reaching veda.

5. Chop the bones of the dead in a Waring Blender.
And then, adding mushrooms, notice the smell
is a condition of the inner nose.

6. The straightest line between two points
is the deepest torque of the present path.

7. A Mohave Vine is a vehicle
that is programmed to self-destruct
as you swag on its burden of desert air.

8. Deliberately awkward or awkwardly deliberate
the unevenness of speech and dream are one.
This fact is best represented by the number 3,
a winging curve that divests itself of content.

9. The present information is mailed to us from Night:
what doesn't happen here doesn't happen there.

10. Time loves us enough
to suck us back into Earth.

11. The window is one of the household senses.
There are three others.

12. Dream is to Death
as Poetry is to Her Vaginal Queendom.

13. The Serpent Mound is a Gargantuan Pudendum,
within which Ants are rumored to carry on
their parabolic lives.

14. Endlessly state the conditions of coming
here, and repeat nothing.

15. Come, let us walk thru this Gothic ogee arch
thinking of its lengthening spinal S
as omen. It lifts us
like a member.

16. Our friend Ogma, 4th century author of the Irish alphabet,
called Ogham, is not dead
as was rumored.

17. Believe nothing.

18. We are heading for a change
which will be perceived as an alteration of tempo
or perhaps of the length of our breeches.
Listen for it while you sleep.

19. Proof has arrived that Jesus did not walk on the water
nor on the alleged Atlantean archipelago just beneath the surface
but on a streak of infra-red emulsion
to which his sandals had been expertly sensitized.

20. ‾‾‾‾ IIII ///// IIII   IIIII   II ‾‾‾‾
          ///// IIII   I   IIIII
says Ogma, who, prefering the dogtail to the dog,
never spells his name with a D (or d').

21. Earth is the principle photo in our family album,
said Mme. Vert. Her voice differs from mine as shades gradate
on Reinhardt's color chart, which is a Möbius strip.

22. The likeness of the image engraves itself
in the track of torsion,
and the Man comes sauntering down.

23. Pedestrians, take note!
The signs are being removed.

24. As for Time, we need it.
The cock of God.

25. The Muse is a four-letter word
of which we cannot seem to get enough.
There has been a marked resistance
to writing It in the history of man.

26. Gnus are animals that seek the secrets
of the open savannahs.

27. In the language of blowholes God is
a highpitched squeal
uttered by Diana with Her Krepid deep
within Her, and Earth is the semen
retained. Can he keep it up?

28. Releasing he seeds the sky with lights.
The stars are past failures.
News that stays news.

29. Counting to 10 he says 7 thrice,
and meditates on a chakra too low
to have a name.

30. The door is the third of the household senses.
There is a thief standing outside. He looks
like a dragonfly, with a thousand crafty eyes.
Your move.

31. You know you are midway in the journey of your life
when you recall the message your mother mumbled
in her sleep. First, she said, as you tried to wake her,
Bring me that case of Coca Cola.
Next, as if her voice sank below her snores,
You will die shortly before your 44th year.
You are being given a decade more than Jesus
because you got a late start. Also:
it won't be on a cross but a mushroom.

32. For the next three days you spend most of your time
circling the block and wondering,
Have I been born yet?
On the fourth day you drink Coke until you vomit.

33. Life is normal,
concluded Jesus in the fateful year.
Why has no one mentioned the butterflies
seeding the air of Golgotha?

34. Om, Stomach of Soma, Phalloid
passing thru the jelly of the eye
and into the Vaseline laden secret
of your highschool sweetheart.
Born a harlot, she left you for a lesbian
and later married your best friend.
The evidence is mounting that there is no such thing
as a circle.

35. *The Son of Man* is the name of a dance
learned by studying the way a vine
climbs the left of Her spreading legs.
No purpose in mind
but to enter.

36. Do you remember now?
asks the stump
upon which our ventriloquogrammic green friend sits
and watches, sits and watches.

37. Three yeas
and a nay.

38. The toilet is the second of the household senses.
And a good one it is.

39. The end is what is most near.
It is always coming.
Daily it is with us.
When it is most here
it is most regular in its vital habits
but it is not a circle.

40. Nor is the Moon. Nor is the Mirror,
Her *gno.* The light begins
where it is seen.

41. I lift the candle and begin to count
the folds of your eye, my love. Your window
is clear,

42. your door opens to the

43. Dolphin passing out the rear
of the Hut. Now I can tell you:
We are the fourth of the household senses.

44. *The roofs look fungusgreen,*
says Jolas, who dwells in Fire.

SOMAPOETICS 58

The stick of which we have spoken,
at perhaps tiresome length, is never
straight. If you toss it like a baton
from hand to hand, it never
repeats itself. If you wave it like a beacon
in the night air, you hear what is never
spoken.

midway

SOMAPOETICS 11   *the metazodiac*

Cousin John sits under a dry oak, his red-lettered R.C. Cola in
his left hand, and watches the penumbral eclipse under the Crab.
He thinks aloud: "The moon reflects only 7% of the light falling
on it, yet has been seen by every member of the human race with
the power of vision." He goes to cross his legs, but crosses his fingers
instead, which allows him to wonder, with a loud though comfortless
literary flair, "By what art this luminiferous ether?" From above,
the hidden voice of Michel Lutin elfishly interjects: "You mistake
the matter, Johnny Appleseed, if you think your 28 optic nerves
have yet perceived 28 spinal rotations worth of Moonstream.
Gaze into the shadow of this residual sheen, and you will see that
you are like a child who has received an Erector Set for Christmas
and, nearing completion of his monument of unaging intellect,
discovers that the last piece is missing. No motor." Shocked by
the sudden presence of the Unintelligible (strictly taboo), Johnathan
turns desperately to the Concrete Poetry of the sky. At first his
mind wanders from intended meditations to The Undersea World
of Jacques Cousteau: A Goatfish crosses the screen, then the
Seasnake (his venom 10 times more potent than the King Cobra's),
and eventually the "500 million year old Wedding of the Chambered
Nautilus." The radius of curvature continually increases in these
spiral mobile homes (he notes), but *can* our molluskan Dantes and
Beatrices survive? The joyous couple wanders back into pre-history,
and the mind, in which their membership obtains, focuses on the
vacant hearth of the American night. Comfortless, yet homelike.
"Climb aboard our phosphorescent ark," chuckles Michel in his
angelic tone, "there are two others we have to include." And next
he instructs the new traveler on long journeys and why they require
long logs. "Like amorous dialogues?" asks John of the crossed
eyes, sea-like bearing his bosom to the Moon. "In a logocarnal
sense," replies the air-borne interlocutor, " like love in the autumnal
lodge, both fiery and ethereal, as dolphins *strike*—emitting somatic
mantra like *fouille, foutre, fokken, ficus*. The fruit of such union,"
he continues in the "middle voice" of intelligence agents of old,
"dutifully *inscribes* in our dendrological notation. It is seen how
limba and leaves cluster; how sails lick etheric-waves without
offsetting metacenter in 14th century pirate-hunting yachts or the

1851 schooner *America* [Pluto stealthily entering Taurus] ; how
John Hawkins conspires with spiteful Neptune to penetrate the
Spanish Armada in 1588; how the torque of Mercury describes
the cybernetic pilot-plan of seamen in periplus, somapathetic with
periploca, that twining Old World wooden vine of the family
Asclepiadaceae; how the 'unparticled matter' of Poe's *Eureka*
propels itself as thought, or how, contrariwise, a dead man inhabits
pure locality; how a convex mirror over the fireplace causes the
room to invaginate voluptuously; how strange 'calls' come, e.g.,
a telephonic voice reaches the top of a spiral staircase in an ex-
lighthouse on Christopher Street, asking the inhabitant, 3:34 P.M.,
25th October, 1972, 'Is this Mr. Coil?,' or, equally curious, how
a "Spirituall Creature, like a pretty girle of 7 or 9 yeares of age,'
named Madimi [alias Marie Delex], should converse during 7 years
of the late 16th c. with Mssrs. Kelley and Dee, as dutifully recorded
in the latter's 'Spirituall Diary'; how the weird language of his
Liber Logaeth still eludes clever linguists; how men and women
in every eon bore themselves to death; how all and everything are."
Madariatza das perifa Lil cabisa . . . , writes Jan in the Record, re-
coiling in alarm: "What have I done?" Alas, during J's lapse into
the unintelligible, kind Michael has abandoned him to fireflies and
indeed to Uranus, that cosmic badass tipping scales in the House
of Marriage. "O Phosphorous," cries J, "O luminous spine of nucleic
torque! Where is the promised Ark, and where the American tongue
to expel the Lording Beast of Word Salad. . . ," etc. Not long
after this comes a man named Henry Payne, bearing news of "the
Summit Conference of the Mohave." "You can call me John,"
says Payne, and: "Jesus! My ears are ringing! Too much talk
surrounding the seamless propulsion of UFO." Meanwhile our
cousin lonesome traveler drifts in the penumbra of awe-inspiring
science, kneeling like an unglazed pot or a pilgrim at the portal of
his own name. Says the newcomer: "Vote was 4 to 3 against
wholesale recomposition. Too risky, what with the three-way
daredevil Pluto (b. 3/13/30) loose in House of Marriage (doubtless
sniffing at Ur-anus, that 198 year old T.V. antenna). Nope, said
the Four, no time to rebuild, with 1984 just around the corner—
i.e., Plutonian Sex and Death garnished with Uranian Law and
Higher Thought! CLEAR THE SKY, chanted the Three, KICK
ASSES AND CLEAN HOUSE! But the Four said, Absolutely
NOT! What we need is new ANGLES! Have you forgotten that
Michael chooses to absent himself? O Noble Three-Chambered

Sun of SOL-OM-ON, look over your shoulder, the News approacheth from behind! When the horny Serpent stares forty feet of Whale in the Sphinx-Eye, hissing, *Hail the Equinox when 1 + 2 + 3 + 4 / adds the infra-ruddy Four*, then, Lady, it's gonna be HOT in the Metazodiac. For the secret is OUT. I.e., Serpens coiling in Fire knows, *Interior is ANTERIOR*, History gathering as Fiery Water in the pressure-cooking gonads of Hydra. And so the Monstrous Seasnake of Orcus rises toward the Scales of Woman. First falls the Virgin to 13, Meta-Master of Torsion, who mounts the Mercurial Staff to Cross-Over into Ultra-Violet, thence to the Manifold Forge of Venus. And PHOSPHORESCENCE, whence the initiatic Leap of the Dolphin, born of the Wedding of Fire and Ether. He climbs, torsioned by Self-enlacing and the Scorpion's Test of Watery Death and the Archer's of Fiery Order—until he comes to the Peaks of Middle Earth. Here our Sea-Goat will *use* or *be used*. And the Great Change? And can Cetus, 14 and Final Participant, carry the Sun to the Belly of the Ram? The Four made no predictions to the grumbling Three, but told of a wandering Lama who sought out Raquel Jodorowsky in Lima, saying: *Long time Star send beam to Himalayas for head of man. No more. Now Andes, for head of woman.*

SOMAPOETICS 12   *the joyous science*

I: THE MATTER

Thanks to the so-called "virtual processes" invoked by Physics
we find ourselves once more magically disposed to cast our gaze
into the future, this time via the crystal balls of Prof. Dobbs:
"Psitrons," those "compresent dispositional factors, which pre-
dispose the future to occur in certain ways"—messengers
from the second time dimension, "perhaps flowing backwards
relative to ours," said Feynman.
                              Only they escape alone to tell
our personal Messenger-RNA the truth about quantum phenomena:
"Under the influence of the perturbing potential, the System
tends to make transitions in all directions at once." Look!
   Virtual Potentialites, Probability Amplitudes
   Swarming particles of imaginary mass
   Interact together like a frictionless gas!

II: THE METHOD

Meditating thus on the surreal world of Nobel Laureates we
glimpse the year 2043 AD: New York City, at a Conference of
International Lognostic Analysts, an expert in Theobiopoetics
lectures on "Concho-Ethological Metamorphs At Play
in the Joyous Science of American Poetry, 1969-1984."
Re: his linking an esoteric brand of paperclips, *Noesting,*
especially their double-coil pattern, to "Metanagogical
Verbal Torsion" in *The 4004 Somapoetics,* a fellow scholar asks,
"But what about the Ventriloquo-Trinitarian View?"
The speaker explains that, in that flavor, Gnowledge
were a cross to which this Somagraph or "Transpirant Torkistem"
be applied or, in one claim, *nailed down* and so writhing
in temporary agony for History's sake. "Moreover," he adds,
"a fleshy Three proves its substance on the betailed and
knotted axon crouched in Four. Thus coinhering in the Lady's
ménage à trois are Melogno, Imagno, and Logno
performing their Virtual Opera. Against great odds
the Third Persona regains his equal part in the plot
by devouring the others, Parent and Mistress,
or rather by Incarnating them in the agonic
exercise in self-figuration.
The net results of this mental operation
are of course the lyrics and satyrics now being studied
with the white wings of time passing."

105

III: THE MEANING

The speaker pauses to nibble his curious phallic vegetable
and gathering his personal power imitates the Oriental Recital:
    "The Child walks out of the egg
    To cross your vision and utter the words:
    Take me into your sexual double-helix
    And forgive us the sin of overstating our case
    But Metafuck is what I have in mind."
"The process of composition," quotes the speaker from
Henry Corbin, "appears to be a hermaneutics of the individual
alert to the secret sympathies between the concrete examples it
juxtaposes," and alluding to "functional investiture," cites:
    "Shells thrown with integrity
    Parabolize themselves like airy seed
    And counterpoint prevailing lines of force
    Disposing the sacred sites of Earth."
And his meta-exegetical reading of the "verse"
A snail is limping thru our egg
describes it as "the sort of Riddle that yields a Name
and makes us color our Albion Pome—
granate-purpura, after the kingly murex,
a rite to multiply the number of red-letter days
possible on *any* calendar that reads the time
as we seafaring folk see it,
scribbled in the green-violet sky of futurity:
the signaling stars and the intermittent firefly
describing itself in cybernetics, to in-
form our minds of the journey at hand.
Anyone with eyes to see who looks now will see
the absence of hidden meaning
in and under the words:
The text itself is the secret
of conversion [A.C. to D.C., Lead into Gold] telling us:
        Attention does not rise
    except as the Sun in us
    comes out of hiding
    from behind the Heart,
                its Path
    disclosing the Map of the World."

*First Chapter: For My Marriage**

1.   *Who is in front of you, during somatachism period?*
A.   The Body. The other one. The twining unto juice.
      What there is, or is there, to go on, or in.
2.   *For what purpose does he come into the classroom?*
A.   To get the word! Greek for body is akin
      to L. *tumere* to swell -- more at THUMB;
      on the other hand, an East Indian leafless vine
      (*Sarcostemma acidum*) of the family *Asclepiadaceae*,
      yielding milky juice; and
      especially a metanoiac mushroom (*Amanita muscaria*,
      Ger *Fliegenpilz*, Russ *mukhomor*, Fre *tue-mouche* or *crapaudin*)—
      Vedic, in the Wassonian Speculation, and much hymned—
      from *su* to press, akin to Av *haoma*, Gk *hyei* it is raining—
      more at SUCK.
3.   *Whom or what does he or she call itself and why?*
A.   Person [a, al] , or what is done alone, like thumb-sucking,
      or depending on the mood to be explicated, *Una figura
      della donna miae*, as Guido says, or *Ewig-weibliche*, as Goethe—
      or Krepid?
4.   *Hamlet? Did you say Hamlet? Who's Hamlet?*
A.   *Amlaghe*, the dog who sniffs the trail of Aster Phaantatos,
      also Asaleny the Little Ass, Wirling the Dwarf, and MOST
      telling: Waril-eghid the Wall-eyed!
5.   *Why in God's name so MANY, or better yet, why TWO eyes?*
A.   One for each direction -- or any number greater than AN
      only -- and their crossways, or causeways:
          (a) The polar cracks in the walls, Left and Right of us;
          (b) The bridge of the nose, what wobbles and glows.
6.   *What do you think when, crossing, you chance to look Heavenward?*
A.   What new Lull in Art is
      needed to Read who or what now Signs
      my rotting name for Star Gazers, those
      bottom-dwelling fish having
      open eyes on top of the head?

*10:34 A.M. Sunday December 17, 1972 (Candlewood Point, Connecticut)—Saturnalia—
352nd day of the year, 9hrs 14mins long, Sunrise in Sagittarius 7:07 A.M., Moonrise
in Taurus 1:43 P.M.—Venus, Mercury and Mars become visible in the East.

7. *Speaking of food and sea, is the raw Oyster Mushroom—*
    that purple seashell lodged in detritus—
    smarter than the cooked?

A. No, you ninny! It's 769 tastebuds behind Oyster-style
    Pleurotus ostreatus, the natural superiority of
    all that is Woman-made by Silver Moonlight; i.e.,
    breaded and fried in olive oil and butter --
        Lo! Aphrodisia rides Her scallop past us!

8. *What is the most painful but fertile visual moment to re-*
    member?

A.   Isis
    Conjuring the Crab-devoured cock of
    Osiris
                Under the distant Nile!

9. *Woe! ah why so far fallen, whence the knife that*
    slices the corpus 14 times, and the brain thrice?

A. Man, this is the DESERT, just look at that SUN!
    Or what do you expect out here on Plate 8 *America a*
    Prophecy "That stony law I stamp to dust: and scatter
    religion abroad / To the four winds as a torn book," or
    as Gerrit of Gloucester says "Alchemists & cooks have the
    same problems, how to manage the heat." *And* potters.
    Amidst the lustful fires, the Conductor waves his Rod
    and we Choristers, astray and sucking up to the audience—
    if it is permissible to speak in this fashion, and *para-*
    contextualize Plotinus, shifting the *noia*
    as gear, urging our Somamobile Eastward to *Ta'wil,* the
    Exegesis that leads the limbs back
    to Her slipknot.

10. *Say, I don't get it, who are you anyway, I mean*
    can a poem BE, without a REAL tone of voice, or can
    there be a poet if you can't find him here?

A. "Being is licit. Hold tight to that."
    -- if I may personate, two-lipped,
    him who gave us his own angelic 11th letter
    to use on a Voice
    or gave it to the Voice
    to use on us.
                By the way, Tap the Tree
    won by 4½ lengths in the 7th at Aquaduct, yesterday, 13th
    Nov. 1972, paid $7.40 and $3.40, before a crowd of 17, 844.
    Jockey: Angel Cordero.

108

11. *Thanks, but I'm no gambler. What I want to know is*
    can a man bathe in the warm wine of Sehnsucht [the hankering
    to Return?] and retain his Manhood and/or social usefulness?
A. Listen, this is what I heard in an old oak stump
    in exchange for tapping a highschool cadence in 3/4 time:
    Between heart-throb and brain-lobe, a hyperspace
    lies in waiting. Lose your shadow, and slip it in.
    Thus I came to know that I am my own sore-spot,
    I have found it, and it is not out on the porch.
    Healing is choice.
12. *Is that the same as to initiate?*
A. No. "To initiate is intransitive." But it follows.
13. *Then what is reflected in Arnolfini's convex mirror?*
A. The Righted hand-clasp of Bride and Groom
    The left-hand curved late-morning window-light.
    Fruit: 3 oranges [?] on table, 1 apple [?] on sill = 4.
    The Artist wearing the much-sought Blue.
    Beside him, the still unidentified "Friend-in-Red."
    Unseen, on mirror-wall, but presumably reversed:
    Johannes de eyck fuit hic 1434
    Likewise the wooden daimon who watches over hands.
14. *What about the 6-branched candlestick*
    with one candle, lit in broad daylight?
A. The turning hexagrams of bivalvic light.
    First: 9 in the 2nd place, No. 7: *Shih | The Army:*
        Water in the Earth: The Power in hiding.
        Binding until all corporeal warfare ends.
        Mars centers in the Man who CAN center the martial.
    Second, thru the Looking Glass: 9 in 5th, No. 8: *Pi/Union:*
        Waters over Earth mingle where they can.
        Know your true collegium, and hold
        It all together.
        Seek the oracles where they are, in and on time.
        The kingly hunt is 3-sided, and all that crosses in front
        Is fourth and free.
    And in the end, where re- and unre-flected
    alike reverse, She,
    K'un, Second and Other,
    receives us who can open
                        Out

SOMAPOETICS 14   *the slipknot*

The moon opening on the black and female sea.
If one adrift so long can trust his power of recall
I believe this is what they name the "moiré effect,"
intractable memory laid across
intractable memory,
                   one man with four women
their eight legs spreading at angles
in his needs, his fig-
leaf
     or the knot he is
tied-up in.
           Stick your head out over the rail,
look down at your life:
from the conical tip of the unburied skull
all the way to wave-patterns,
                 water-on-the-brain,
                         grids

aspin
      on the spinal column,
the venereal web of Ariadne that
we are gathering in the long sleep of
history, the lamb
we are roasting whole.
            The tongue turns green
talking to street-arabs, birds and
sufi vagrants at the Court of Miracles
                 on the hunch
Villon will show.
He will serenade the clairvoyant oppressed
and teach their earthy anthropos to
jostle itself with
           "irrepressible inner laughter"
and lay bare this
chaste affair of
thinking
our way clear.

GLOSSARY

A.C./D.C.: The androgenous circuitry of the First House.

Adam's Fortunate Fall: Anterior usage, according to interior evidence: "As the sower soweth the word / So the mind walks / And climbing to the point / Of a Virtual Peak / Is slain." [Kos]

Amrita: A mellifluous, deathless drink that pleases and lubricates the mother tongue.

Arnolfini of Lucca: Alledged subject (with Bride) of Jan Van Eyck's notorious portrait; supposed member of so-called Confraternity of the Dry Tree; and reportedly in Bruges (1420-72), a city whose courtyards have gates, bridges and alleyways that lead into courtyards that lead on inward. The subject of the picture by "John of the Oak" (1434) is clearly of a kind with the speaker of that marvellous Romance, "The Chymical Wedding of Christian Rosencreutz" (1616).

Divine: The opposite of divide.

Heresy: The saving grace of Junaid of Baghdad, who says: "None reaches the rank of Truth until a thousand honest people testify that he is a heretic."

Hilaritas: 1. [L.] Gaity, as in [Prov.] "gai saber," e.g.: "gaity transfiguring all that dread" [Yeats]. 2. The fourth "thing needed for beauty," added to the Aquinian three, "integritas, consonantia, claritas," (i.e., in the words of Dedalus: "Wholeness, harmony, radiance"). 3. Delight, a shining mood or mode, a showing forth, a radiant event that lightens the mind, one instant in the life of a flamebrain (Erigena: "lux enim ignis est accidens," Canto LXXXIII), as a kind of light that spirals within water: Claritas opening like a bud of Anthurium, revealing the yellow tail that was hid. 4. As Uncle George says, one sometimes experiences "irrepressible inner laughter" when witnessing an accident of the Cosmic Law of Falling and Catching Up.

Krepid: (also Crepidinous, etc.): The name a voice whispers to itself using the third mouth while the other two wear each other in 69. Polar logic? Crepidam? Uncle George reckons a man wears shoes to keep his feet out of the mud.

Landscape: A kind of portaiture showing the opposite of "escape."

Law of Conservation of Somapoeia: The principle that nothing that is thought, said or otherwise known in direct connection with something or someone outside the self can ever be lost or destroyed but is forever "written" in the great self-intercoursing body (Soma) of the knowable universe. The library is open (at the mouth and at the end) but transportation must be provided by the reader.

Lognosis: Knowing the Female Word carnally.

Metanoia: [fr. Gk. "change" + "mind-activity"] The outcome [see Proteotelesis] of practicing Metapoeia [q.v.].

Metapoeia: The practice of making change in and thru language by use of any one (or more) structural principle(s) governing the apparently limitless resources of human Babel, particularly as "grasped" in the state of Troponoia [q.v.].

Ne sutor ultra crepidam: [L.] "Cobbler, stick to your last," a synchronistic cry from the Behmenistic shoes of Goerlitz to the Sufic sandals of the Middle Orient.

Pan: 1. The container used over open Fire. 2. All and Nothing, going by many names: e.g., King Garlic, Hipelpipel, or any about whom it was said: "Tell Dilldrum that Doldrum is dead." 3. Krepid?

Parabolic: The curved presence of meaning, known from the perceptual vantage of a stone, which has been thrown and is now midair, traveling to unknown terrain.

Perspective by Interference: The technic of "seeing thru or into by reflexive striking or cross-boring," and the key to any "combinatory art": e.g., The Ghent Polyptych of Van Eyck, many-windowed like the Argus Pheasant, whose 20 panels (8 exterior, 7 + 5 interior) present a single self-interfering image with the techtonics of a house by Magritte. Likewise Persian pictures of the Ka'aba in which all elements are represented "in the present," "in each case perpendicularly to the axis of the viewer's vision" [Henry Corbin].

Physiognogram: A Concrete Somamudra [q.v.], or a Dancing Child of Blake's Illumination, or a lesson in how to sit on the page and know the sense of crawling on the Ear- and Brain-lobes, until a Mighty Shape appears.

Prospero: Metacarnate name of John Dee, inventor of the Flying Crab, which lifted Trygaeus the vine-dresser from stage to the "Palace of Zeus" in Aristophenes' "Pax."

Proteotelesis: The end of change changing in the end.

Sententia-Amphibologia: A way of thinking that feels like riding the two-way stallion of Chance. Four hoofs hit the ground, but only three are heard, and Mallarme passes the dice to Magritte.

Somagram: A Physiogngram [q.v.] in conference with the planet Mercury [conjunct with Venus in opposition to Mars quincuncial with jovial Jupiter, causing Serpens to poke his horny nose up into Venus, thereby giving rise to the Leaping Dolphin who turns on the Metazodiac. Note the carnal relations between SOMAPOETICS 10 and 11, where No. 10, our fortune as marriage, presents the elongation of Mercury as witnessed from ark-deck.

Somamudra: 1. The art of picturing a body in which knowledge has the upper hand. 2. Tibetan PHYAG-RGYA-MA: taking hold of, as Yoni grasps Lingam (in principle and in fact) and as the ether is sealed with light, revealing Invigorating Food—sweet Amrita [q.v.], woman, Venereal fruit of Soma Activity. 3. A Great Doing, e.g.: Rub you hands like tightfisted Shylock gazing at a priceless copy of the Sepher Yetzirah; reluctantly shift attention to the circular sweep of your palms, allowing a heal-toe freewheeling torque: now LIFT!

Star-Seeing: To see stars is to experience bright flashing sensations, an activity regarded by Mohave Masters as a stage of initiation into the inevitable seduction of particles by waves.

Trinity of Active Moods: The Leer of Pan, the Beatific Smile of Buddha, and the Torsion of Christ-Agonystes.

Tropia: Deviation of eye from normal or ordinary line of vision.

Troponoia: A state of being in which the prehensile mind operates at high torque, properly the proteotelic turnout of an act of Tropopoeia [q.v.]. (For a clearer picture, visualize the mind of Leonardo imagining an airscrew and taking account of the torque or moment of air force on its blades; or hold in the "middle hand" of your transverbal imagination the full-bodied figure of a twining vine, noting like D'Arcy Thompson the operative torsion, and then allow yourself for an "instant of time" to become what you behold.)

Tropopoeia: "Torsion-making within the mother tongue" or any other translation of a hypothetical Vedic term covering the general category of poesis in which Soma-poeia is a specific case. Related to [ch.] Hsin[1], Confucian "Making it new" [fr. growth-process in "marshy plant"], i.e., making it turn, or it makes you turn, or [in Somapoeic middle voice] turning + making + I + you are (is/am) happening, as "verse."

112

Ventriloquogram: What is heard as thinking to be seen in many a throat cocked open in clear torque. Example: The talkative ghost of Charlie MacCarthy is seen haunting the vortex of history amidst an overwhelming sound of martial flushing, and prevails against the odds.

Vision: What in the long run cannot be faked.

War: Raw backwards. Historical narcolepsy. One way or another, we get faced around.

[Continued in Book Two]

A NOTE ON COUNTING AND KNOWING WHAT COUNTS

I cannot resist a comparison of our situation with that great Platonic work in Biopoesis where Socrates says: "One, two, three—but where, my dear Timaeus, is the fourth of those guests of yesterday who were to entertain me today?" From the present vantage I see these possible answers to the Philospher's question: (1) The reader who chooses to excuse himself from the day's festivities. (2) Anyone able to prove that four comes before three, in which case (he reasons) why bother to make an appearance just to please Philosophy? (3) Code no. 007, of which there is one in every age—such as Dr. John Dee (b. July 13, 1527), Secret Agent for Elizabeth I, who is busy today: stirring up trouble in Bohemia; composing a horoscope for Edmund Spenser; or writing the MONAS HIEROGLYPHICA in the thirteen days beginning Jan, 13, 1564. (4) The genetic informant who does not appear to supply information on this occasion [cf. the researches of Dr. H. Bialy]. (5) One whom we've only recently begun to consider; however, the time is not ripe for open speculation, despite the new atmosphere of frankness in which Dr. Crick finds it possible to hypothesize, on the basis of genetics, that Life was "planted" on Earth by extraterrestrials. I am by no means suggesting that the mysterious fourth persona was an "ancient astronaut" traveling in a saucer-shaped "Chariot of the gods;" but a traveller he was—and one imagines the Chariot of Genius, gathering momentum along the road to Canterbury, must at a certain point become airborne. Are we ready, perhaps, to speak of the fifth persona, also missing? Have we come at last to the matter of woman, our Venus rising?